MznLnx

Missing Links Exam Preps

Exam Prep for

Marketing and E-Commerce

Miller & Jentz, 1st Edition

The MznLnx Exam Prep is your link from the texbook and lecture to your exams.
The MznLnx Exam Preps are unauthorized and comprehensive reviews of your textbooks.

All material provided by MznLnx and Rico Publications (c) 2010
Textbook publishers and textbook authors do not particpate in or contribute to these reviews.

MznLnx

Rico
Publications

Exam Prep for Marketing and E-Commerce
1st Edition
Miller & Jentz

Publisher: Raymond Houge
Assistant Editor: Michael Rouger
Text and Cover Designer: Lisa Buckner
Marketing Manager: Sara Swagger
Project Manager, Editorial Production: Jerry Emerson
Art Director: Vernon Lowerui

Product Manager: Dave Mason
Editorial Assitant: Rachel Guzmanji
Pedagogy: Debra Long
Cover Image: Jim Reed/Getty Images
Text and Cover Printer: City Printing, Inc.
Compositor: Media Mix, Inc.

(c) 2010 Rico Publications
ALL RIGHTS RESERVED. No part of this work covered by the copyright may be reproduced or used in any form or by an means--graphic, electronic, or mechanical, including photocopying, recording, taping, Web distribution, information storage, and retrieval systems, or in any other manner--without the written permission of the publisher.

Printed in the United States
ISBN:

For more information about our products, contact us at:
Dave.Mason@RicoPublications.com

For permission to use material from this text or product, submit a request online to:
Dave.Mason@RicoPublications.com

Contents

CHAPTER 1
Introduction to Law — 1

CHAPTER 2
Resolution of Disputes — 8

CHAPTER 3
E-Commerce and Dispute Resolution — 14

CHAPTER 4
Cyber Torts and Crimes — 20

CHAPTER 5
Intellectual Property—Patents and Copyrights — 32

CHAPTER 6
Intellectual Property—Trademarks, Cyber Marks, and Trade Secrets — 40

CHAPTER 7
Online Marketing — 49

CHAPTER 8
Consumer Protection and Privacy Issues — 57

ANSWER KEY — 68

TO THE STUDENT

COMPREHENSIVE

The *MznLnx* Exam Prep series is designed to help you pass your exams. Editors at MznLnx review your textbooks and then prepare these practice exams to help you master the textbook material. Unlike study guides, workbooks, and practice tests provided by the texbook publisher and textbook authors, *MznLnx* gives you **all** of the material in each chapter in exam form, not just samples, so you can be sure to nail your exam.

MECHANICAL

The MznLnx Exam Prep series creates exams that will help you learn the subject matter as well as test you on your understanding. Each question is designed to help you master the concept. Just working through the exams, you gain an understanding of the subject--its a simple mechanical process that produces success.

INTEGRATED STUDY GUIDE AND REVIEW

MznLnx is not just a set of exams designed to test you, its also a comprehensive review of the subject content. Each exam question is also a review of the concept, making sure that you will get the answer correct without having to go to other sources of material. You learn as you go! Its the easiest way to pass an exam.

HUMOR

Studying can be tedious and dry. MznLnx's instructional design includes moderate humor within the exam questions on occassion, to break the tedium and revitalize the brain

Chapter 1. Introduction to Law

1. In the law of Remedy, an order of _____ is an order of the court which requires a party to perform a specific act, usually what is stated in a contract. While _____ can be in the form of any type of forced action, it is usually used to complete a previously established transaction, thus being the most effective remedy in protecting the expectation interest of the innocent party to a contract. It is usually the opposite of a prohibitory injunction but there are mandatory injunctions which have a similar effect to _____.
   a. Competition law
   b. Priority right
   c. Singapore Treaty on the Law of Trademarks
   d. Specific performance

2. _____, a form of alternative dispute resolution (ADR), is a legal technique for the resolution of disputes outside the courts, wherein the parties to a dispute refer it to one or more persons (the 'arbitrators', 'arbiters' or 'arbitral tribunal'), by whose decision (the 'award') they agree to be bound. It is a settlement technique in which a third party reviews the case and imposes a decision that is legally binding for both sides. Other forms of ADR include mediation (a form of settlement negotiation facilitated by a neutral third party) and non-binding resolution by experts.
   a. AMAX
   b. Arbitration
   c. ACNielsen
   d. ADTECH

3. _____ is a form of social influence. It is the process of guiding people toward the adoption of an idea, attitude, or action by rational and symbolic (though not always logical) means. It is strategy of problem-solving relying on 'appeals' rather than coercion.
   a. Power III
   b. 180SearchAssistant
   c. 6-3-5 Brainwriting
   d. Persuasion

4. _____ is systematic determination of merit, worth, and significance of something or someone using criteria against a set of standards. _____ often is used to characterize and appraise subjects of interest in a wide range of human enterprises, including the arts, criminal justice, foundations and non-profit organizations, government, health care, and other human services.

Depending on the topic of interest, there are professional groups which look to the quality and rigor of the _____ process.

a. Evaluation
b. AMAX
c. ACNielsen
d. ADTECH

5. _____ are legal property rights over creations of the mind, both artistic and commercial, and the corresponding fields of law. Under _____ law, owners are granted certain exclusive rights to a variety of intangible assets, such as musical, literary, and artistic works; ideas, discoveries and inventions; and words, phrases, symbols, and designs. Common types of _____ include copyrights, trademarks, patents, industrial design rights and trade secrets.

a. Elasticity
b. Opinion leadership
c. ACNielsen
d. Intellectual property

6. The U.S. _____ is an agency of the United States Department of Health and Human Services and is responsible for regulating and supervising the safety of foods, dietary supplements, drugs, vaccines, biological medical products, blood products, medical devices, radiation-emitting devices, veterinary products, and cosmetics. The FDA also enforces section 361 of the Public Health Service Act and the associated regulations, including sanitation requirements on interstate travel as well as specific rules for control of disease on products ranging from pet turtles to semen donations for assisted reproductive medicine techniques.

The FDA is an agency within the United States Department of Health and Human Services responsible for protecting and promoting the nation's public health.

a. 6-3-5 Brainwriting
b. Power III
c. 180SearchAssistant
d. Food and Drug Administration

7. The _____ of the United States Constitution, which is part of the Bill of Rights, was ratified on December 15, 1791. The _____ restates the Constitution's principle of Federalism by providing that powers not granted to the national government nor prohibited to the states are reserved to the states or the people.

The _____ is similar to an earlier provision of the Articles of Confederation: 'Each state retains its sovereignty, freedom, and independence, and every power, jurisdiction, and right, which is not by this Confederation expressly delegated to the United States, in Congress assembled.' After the Constitution was ratified, some wanted to add a similar amendment limiting the federal government to powers 'expressly' delegated, which would have denied implied powers.

a. Brand piracy
b. Social Norms Approach
c. Fair trade law
d. Tenth Amendment

8. A _____ is a relatively new executive level position at a corporation, company, organization typically reporting directly to the CEO or board of directors. The _____ is responsible for a brand's image, experience, and promise, and propagating it throughout all aspects of the company. The brand officer oversees marketing, advertising, design, public relations and customer service departments.

a. Financial analyst
b. Power III
c. Chief executive officer
d. Chief brand officer

9. The _____ is an independent agency of the United States government, created, directed, and empowered by Congressional statute , and with the majority of its commissioners appointed by the current President.

a. 180SearchAssistant
b. Power III
c. 6-3-5 Brainwriting
d. Federal Communications Commission

10. The _____ is an independent agency of the United States government, established in 1914 by the _____ Act. Its principal mission is the promotion of 'consumer protection' and the elimination and prevention of what regulators perceive to be harmfully 'anti-competitive' business practices, such as coercive monopoly.

The _____ Act was one of President Wilson's major acts against trusts.

a. Power III
b. 180SearchAssistant
c. 6-3-5 Brainwriting
d. Federal Trade Commission

11. The U.S. _____ is an independent agency of the United States government which holds primary responsibility for enforcing the federal securities laws and regulating the securities industry, the nation's stock and options exchanges, and other electronic securities markets. The SEC was created by section 4 of the Securities Exchange Act of 1934 (now codified as 15 U.S.C. Â§ 78d and commonly referred to as the 1934 Act).

Chapter 1. Introduction to Law

   a. Power III
   b. Securities and Exchange Commission
   c. 180SearchAssistant
   d. 6-3-5 Brainwriting

12. _____ refers to 'controlling human or societal behaviour by rules or restrictions.' _____ can take many forms: legal restrictions promulgated by a government authority, self-_____, social _____, co-_____ and market _____. One can consider _____ as actions of conduct imposing sanctions (such as a fine.) This action of administrative law, or implementing regulatory law, may be contrasted with statutory or case law.
   a. CAN-SPAM
   b. Rule of four
   c. Non-conventional trademark
   d. Regulation

13. Regulation refers to 'controlling human or societal behaviour by rules or restrictions.' Regulation can take many forms: legal restrictions promulgated by a government authority, self-regulation, social regulation (e.g. norms), co-regulation and market regulation. One can consider regulation as actions of conduct imposing sanctions (such as a fine.) This action of administrative law, or implementing _____ law, may be contrasted with statutory or case law.
   a. Robinson-Patman Act
   b. Privacy law
   c. Regulatory
   d. Right to Financial Privacy Act

14. The _____ is the de facto national library of the United States and the research arm of the United States Congress. Located in three buildings in Washington, D.C., it is the largest library in the world by shelf space and holds the largest number of books. The head of the Library is the Librarian of Congress, currently James H. Billington.
   a. 180SearchAssistant
   b. Power III
   c. 6-3-5 Brainwriting
   d. Library of Congress

15. _____ is an advertisement in which a particular product specifically mentions a competitor by name for the express purpose of showing why the competitor is inferior to the product naming it.

This should not be confused with parody advertisements, where a fictional product is being advertised for the purpose of poking fun at the particular advertisement, nor should it be confused with the use of a coined brand name for the purpose of comparing the product without actually naming an actual competitor. ('Wikipedia tastes better and is less filling than the Encyclopedia Galactica.')

Chapter 1. Introduction to Law 5

In the 1980s, during what has been referred to as the cola wars, soft-drink manufacturer Pepsi ran a series of advertisements where people, caught on hidden camera, in a blind taste test, chose Pepsi over rival Coca-Cola.

a. GL-70
b. Heavy-up
c. Cost per conversion
d. Comparative advertising

16. The _____ is a very large set of interlinked hypertext documents accessed via the Internet. With a Web browser, one can view Web pages that may contain text, images, videos, and other multimedia and navigate between them using hyperlinks. Using concepts from earlier hypertext systems, the _____ was begun in 1992 by the English physicist Sir Tim Berners-Lee, now the Director of the _____ Consortium, and Robert Cailliau, a Belgian computer scientist, while both were working at CERN in Geneva, Switzerland.
  a. 180SearchAssistant
  b. Power III
  c. 6-3-5 Brainwriting
  d. World Wide Web

17. _____ is the statutory or written law that governs rights and obligations of those who are subject to it. _____ defines the legal relationship of people with other people or between them and the state. _____ stands in contrast to procedural law, which comprises the rules by which a court hears and determines what happens in civil or criminal proceedings.
  a. Leading question
  b. Power III
  c. Contract price
  d. Substantive law

18. Electronic commerce, commonly known as _____ or eCommerce, consists of the buying and selling of products or services over electronic systems such as the Internet and other computer networks. The amount of trade conducted electronically has grown extraordinarily with wide-spread Internet usage. A wide variety of commerce is conducted in this way, spurring and drawing on innovations in electronic funds transfer, supply chain management, Internet marketing, online transaction processing, electronic data interchange (EDI), inventory management systems, and automated data collection systems.
  a. ACNielsen
  b. E-commerce
  c. AMAX
  d. ADTECH

Chapter 1. Introduction to Law

19. The _____ is a compilation and codification of the general and permanent federal law of the United States. It contains 50 titles and is published every six years by the Office of the Law Revision Counsel of the US House of Representatives.

The official text of an Act of Congress is that of the 'enrolled bill' (traditionally printed on parchment) presented to the President for his signature or disapproval.

   a. ADTECH
   b. AMAX
   c. ACNielsen
   d. United States Code

20. _____ is a term commonly used to describe commerce transactions between businesses like the one between a manufacturer and a wholesaler or a wholesaler and a retailer i.e both the buyer and the seller are business entity.This is unlike business-to-consumers (B2C) which involve a business entity and end consumer, or business-to-government (B2G) which involve a business entity and government.

The volume of B2B transactions is much higher than the volume of B2C transactions. The primary reason for this is that in a typical supply chain there will be many B2B transactions involving subcomponent or raw materials, and only one B2C transaction, specifically sale of the finished product to the end customer.

   a. Disruptive technology
   b. Social marketing
   c. Customer relationship management
   d. Business-to-business

21. A _____ is a set of exclusive rights granted by a State to an inventor or his assignee for a limited period of time in exchange for a disclosure of an invention.

The procedure for granting _____s, the requirements placed on the _____ee and the extent of the exclusive rights vary widely between countries according to national laws and international agreements. Typically, however, a _____ application must include one or more claims defining the invention which must be new, inventive, and useful or industrially applicable.

   a. Product liability
   b. Patent
   c. Reasonable person standard
   d. Foreign Corrupt Practices Act

Chapter 1. Introduction to Law

22. In computing, a _____ is a type of Uniform Resource Identifier (URI) that specifies where an identified resource is available and the mechanism for retrieving it. In popular usage and in many technical documents and verbal discussions it is often incorrectly used as a synonym for URI. In popular language, a _____ is also referred to as a Web address.

   a. AMAX
   b. ADTECH
   c. ACNielsen
   d. Uniform Resource Locator

23. _____ is a technique used in propaganda and advertising. Also known as association, this is a technique of projecting positive or negative qualities (praise or blame) of a person, entity, object, or value (an individual, group, organization, nation, patriotism, etc.) to another in order to make the second more acceptable or to discredit it.

   a. Micro ads
   b. Sexism,
   c. Supplier
   d. Transfer

24. In law, a _____ is a ruling issued by an appellate court with multiple judges in which the decision rendered was made by the court acting as a whole, anonymously. In contrast to regular opinions, the decision does not list the individual judge responsible for authoring the decision.

   _____s are not the only type of decision that can reflect the opinion of the court.

   a. 6-3-5 Brainwriting
   b. Power III
   c. Per curiam decision
   d. 180SearchAssistant

Chapter 2. Resolution of Disputes

1. _____ exists where two or more courts from different systems simultaneously have jurisdiction over a specific case. This situation leads to forum shopping, as parties will try to have their lawsuit heard in the court that they perceive will be most favorable to them.

   In the United States, _____ exists to the extent that the Constitution of the United States permits U.S. federal courts to hear actions that can also be heard by U.S. state courts.

   a. Power III
   b. 180SearchAssistant
   c. 6-3-5 Brainwriting
   d. Concurrent jurisdiction

2. In law, a _____ is a question which must be answered by reference to facts and evidence, and inferences arising from those facts. Such a question is distinct from a question of law, which must be answered by applying relevant legal principles. The answer to a _____ is usually dependent on particular circumstances or factual situations.

   a. Power III
   b. 180SearchAssistant
   c. 6-3-5 Brainwriting
   d. Question of fact

3. A _____ is a relatively new executive level position at a corporation, company, organization typically reporting directly to the CEO or board of directors. The _____ is responsible for a brand's image, experience, and promise, and propagating it throughout all aspects of the company. The brand officer oversees marketing, advertising, design, public relations and customer service departments.

   a. Financial analyst
   b. Chief executive officer
   c. Power III
   d. Chief brand officer

4. The _____ is a Supreme Court of the United States practice that permits four of the nine justices to grant a writ of certiorari. This is done specifically to prevent a majority of the court from controlling all the cases it agrees to hear.

   The _____ is not required by the Constitution, any law, or even the Supreme Court's own published rules.

   a. Priority right
   b. Wheeler-Lea Act
   c. Collective trade mark
   d. Rule of four

Chapter 2. Resolution of Disputes

5. The _____ is a very large set of interlinked hypertext documents accessed via the Internet. With a Web browser, one can view Web pages that may contain text, images, videos, and other multimedia and navigate between them using hyperlinks. Using concepts from earlier hypertext systems, the _____ was begun in 1992 by the English physicist Sir Tim Berners-Lee, now the Director of the _____ Consortium, and Robert Cailliau, a Belgian computer scientist, while both were working at CERN in Geneva, Switzerland.
   a. World Wide Web
   b. 6-3-5 Brainwriting
   c. Power III
   d. 180SearchAssistant

6. _____ is the ability of an individual or group to seclude themselves or information about themselves and thereby reveal themselves selectively. The boundaries and content of what is considered private differ among cultures and individuals, but share basic common themes. _____ is sometimes related to anonymity, the wish to remain unnoticed or unidentified in the public realm.
   a. Power III
   b. 180SearchAssistant
   c. Privacy
   d. 6-3-5 Brainwriting

7. _____ includes dispute resolution processes and techniques that fall outside of the government judicial process. Despite historic resistance to _____ by both parties and their advocates, _____ has gained widespread acceptance among both the general public and the legal profession in recent years. In fact, some courts now require some parties to resort to _____ of some type, usually mediation, before permitting the parties' cases to be tried.
   a. AMAX
   b. ACNielsen
   c. ADTECH
   d. Alternative dispute resolution

8. _____, a form of alternative dispute resolution (ADR), is a legal technique for the resolution of disputes outside the courts, wherein the parties to a dispute refer it to one or more persons (the 'arbitrators', 'arbiters' or 'arbitral tribunal'), by whose decision (the 'award') they agree to be bound. It is a settlement technique in which a third party reviews the case and imposes a decision that is legally binding for both sides. Other forms of ADR include mediation (a form of settlement negotiation facilitated by a neutral third party) and non-binding resolution by experts.
   a. ACNielsen
   b. ADTECH
   c. AMAX
   d. Arbitration

Chapter 2. Resolution of Disputes

9. _____ is systematic determination of merit, worth, and significance of something or someone using criteria against a set of standards. _____ often is used to characterize and appraise subjects of interest in a wide range of human enterprises, including the arts, criminal justice, foundations and non-profit organizations, government, health care, and other human services.

Depending on the topic of interest, there are professional groups which look to the quality and rigor of the _____ process.

   a. ADTECH
   b. ACNielsen
   c. AMAX
   d. Evaluation

10. In statistics, _____ has two related meanings:

   - the arithmetic _____
   - the expected value of a random variable, which is also called the population _____.

It is sometimes stated that the '_____' _____s average. This is incorrect if '_____' is taken in the specific sense of 'arithmetic _____' as there are different types of averages: the _____, median, and mode. For instance, average house prices almost always use the median value for the average. These three types of averages are all measures of locations.

   a. Heteroskedastic
   b. Standard normal distribution
   c. Confidence interval
   d. Mean

11. _____, a form of alternative dispute resolution (ADR) or 'appropriate dispute resolution', aims to assist two (or more) disputants in reaching an agreement. The parties themselves determine the conditions of any settlements reached-- rather than accepting something imposed by a third party. The disputes may involve (as parties) states, organizations, communities, individuals or other representatives with a vested interest in the outcome.
   a. Fair trade law
   b. Mediation
   c. Magnuson-Moss Warranty Act
   d. Specific Performance

12. An _____ is a determination on the merits by an arbitration tribunal in an arbitration, and is analogous to a judgment in a court of law. It is referred to as an 'award' even where all of the claimant's claims fail (and thus no money needs to be paid by either party), or the award is of a non-monetary nature.

Chapter 2. Resolution of Disputes

Although _____s are characteristically an award of damages against a party, tribunals usually have a range of remedies that can form a part of the award.

a. ADTECH
b. AMAX
c. ACNielsen
d. Arbitration award

13. The _____ is one of the uniform acts that attempt to harmonize the law in force in the fifty U.S. states.
a. AMAX
b. ADTECH
c. ACNielsen
d. Uniform Arbitration Act

14. The most important feature of a contract is that one party makes an _____ for an arrangement that another accepts. This can be called a 'concurrence of wills' or 'ad idem' (meeting of the minds) of two or more parties. The concept is somewhat contested.
a. ACNielsen
b. AMAX
c. Offer
d. ADTECH

15. The _____ of 1967, Pub. L. No. 90-202, 81 Stat. 602 (Dec. 15, 1967), codified as Chapter 14 of Title 29 of the United States Code, 29 U.S.C. § 621 through 29 U.S.C. § 634 (ADEA), prohibits employment discrimination against persons 40 years of age or older in the United States. The law also sets standards for pensions and benefits provided by employers and requires that information about the needs of older workers be provided to the general public.
a. ADTECH
b. Age Discrimination in Employment Act
c. ACNielsen
d. AMAX

16. _____ is a contract between two parties, one being the employer and the other being the employee. An employee may be defined as: 'A person in the service of another under any contract of hire, express or implied, oral or written, where the employer has the power or right to control and direct the employee in the material details of how the work is to be performed.' Black's Law Dictionary page 471 (5th ed. 1979.)

Chapter 2. Resolution of Disputes

a. Employment
b. ACNielsen
c. AMAX
d. ADTECH

17. _____ is a broad label that refers to any individuals or households that use goods and services generated within the economy. The concept of a _____ is used in different contexts, so that the usage and significance of the term may vary.

A _____ is a person who uses any product or service.

a. 6-3-5 Brainwriting
b. 180SearchAssistant
c. Consumer
d. Power III

18. _____ is a form of government regulation which protects the interests of consumers. For example, a government may require businesses to disclose detailed information about products--particularly in areas where safety or public health is an issue, such as food. _____ is linked to the idea of consumer rights (that consumers have various rights as consumers), and to the formation of consumer organizations which help consumers make better choices in the marketplace.

a. Trademark dilution
b. Federal Bureau of Investigation
c. Consumer Protection
d. Sound trademark

19. _____, commonly known as e-commerce or eCommerce, consists of the buying and selling of products or services over electronic systems such as the Internet and other computer networks. The amount of trade conducted electronically has grown extraordinarily with wide-spread Internet usage. A wide variety of commerce is conducted in this way, spurring and drawing on innovations in electronic funds transfer, supply chain management, Internet marketing, online transaction processing, electronic data interchange (EDI), inventory management systems, and automated data collection systems.

a. ADTECH
b. AMAX
c. ACNielsen
d. Electronic Commerce

20. _____ refers to 'controlling human or societal behaviour by rules or restrictions.' _____ can take many forms: legal restrictions promulgated by a government authority, self-_____, social _____, co-_____ and market _____. One can consider _____ as actions of conduct imposing sanctions (such as a fine.) This action of administrative law, or implementing regulatory law, may be contrasted with statutory or case law.
   a. Rule of four
   b. Regulation
   c. CAN-SPAM
   d. Non-conventional trademark

Chapter 3. E-Commerce and Dispute Resolution

1. _____ is a term commonly used to describe commerce transactions between businesses like the one between a manufacturer and a wholesaler or a wholesaler and a retailer i.e both the buyer and the seller are business entity. This is unlike business-to-consumers (B2C) which involve a business entity and end consumer, or business-to-government (B2G) which involve a business entity and government.

The volume of B2B transactions is much higher than the volume of B2C transactions. The primary reason for this is that in a typical supply chain there will be many B2B transactions involving subcomponent or raw materials, and only one B2C transaction, specifically sale of the finished product to the end customer.

   a. Business-to-business
   b. Disruptive technology
   c. Customer relationship management
   d. Social marketing

2. _____ describes activities of businesses serving end consumers with products and/or services.

An example of a B2C transaction would be a person buying a pair of shoes from a retailer. The transactions that led to the shoes being available for purchase, that is the purchase of the leather, laces, rubber, etc.

   a. Corporate capabilities package
   b. Societal marketing
   c. Demand generation
   d. Business-to-consumer

3. _____ is a broad label that refers to any individuals or households that use goods and services generated within the economy. The concept of a _____ is used in different contexts, so that the usage and significance of the term may vary.

A _____ is a person who uses any product or service.

   a. 6-3-5 Brainwriting
   b. Power III
   c. Consumer
   d. 180SearchAssistant

4. Electronic commerce, commonly known as _____ or eCommerce, consists of the buying and selling of products or services over electronic systems such as the Internet and other computer networks. The amount of trade conducted electronically has grown extraordinarily with wide-spread Internet usage. A wide variety of commerce is conducted in this way, spurring and drawing on innovations in electronic funds transfer, supply chain management, Internet marketing, online transaction processing, electronic data interchange (EDI), inventory management systems, and automated data collection systems.

a. ADTECH
b. AMAX
c. ACNielsen
d. E-commerce

5. The _____ is a very large set of interlinked hypertext documents accessed via the Internet. With a Web browser, one can view Web pages that may contain text, images, videos, and other multimedia and navigate between them using hyperlinks. Using concepts from earlier hypertext systems, the _____ was begun in 1992 by the English physicist Sir Tim Berners-Lee, now the Director of the _____ Consortium, and Robert Cailliau, a Belgian computer scientist, while both were working at CERN in Geneva, Switzerland.
   a. World Wide Web
   b. 6-3-5 Brainwriting
   c. 180SearchAssistant
   d. Power III

6. The _____ is an independent agency of the United States government, established in 1914 by the _____ Act. Its principal mission is the promotion of 'consumer protection' and the elimination and prevention of what regulators perceive to be harmfully 'anti-competitive' business practices, such as coercive monopoly.

The _____ Act was one of President Wilson's major acts against trusts.

   a. 6-3-5 Brainwriting
   b. Power III
   c. 180SearchAssistant
   d. Federal Trade Commission

7. _____ is a form of government regulation which protects the interests of consumers. For example, a government may require businesses to disclose detailed information about products--particularly in areas where safety or public health is an issue, such as food. _____ is linked to the idea of consumer rights (that consumers have various rights as consumers), and to the formation of consumer organizations which help consumers make better choices in the marketplace.
   a. Federal Bureau of Investigation
   b. Trademark dilution
   c. Sound trademark
   d. Consumer Protection

Chapter 3. E-Commerce and Dispute Resolution

8. _____, commonly known as e-commerce or eCommerce, consists of the buying and selling of products or services over electronic systems such as the Internet and other computer networks. The amount of trade conducted electronically has grown extraordinarily with wide-spread Internet usage. A wide variety of commerce is conducted in this way, spurring and drawing on innovations in electronic funds transfer, supply chain management, Internet marketing, online transaction processing, electronic data interchange (EDI), inventory management systems, and automated data collection systems.
   a. Electronic Commerce
   b. ADTECH
   c. AMAX
   d. ACNielsen

9. A _____ or domain name (TLD) is the highest level of domain names in the root zone of the Domain Name System of the Internet. For all domains in lower levels, it is the last part of the domain name, that is, the label that follows the last dot of a fully qualified domain name. For example, in the domain name `www.example.com`, the _____ is `com` (or `COM`, as domain names are not case-sensitive.)
   a. Domain name drop list
   b. Domain name speculation
   c. Typosquatting
   d. Top-level domain

10. _____, a form of alternative dispute resolution (ADR), is a legal technique for the resolution of disputes outside the courts, wherein the parties to a dispute refer it to one or more persons (the 'arbitrators', 'arbiters' or 'arbitral tribunal'), by whose decision (the 'award') they agree to be bound. It is a settlement technique in which a third party reviews the case and imposes a decision that is legally binding for both sides. Other forms of ADR include mediation (a form of settlement negotiation facilitated by a neutral third party) and non-binding resolution by experts.
   a. ACNielsen
   b. ADTECH
   c. AMAX
   d. Arbitration

11. _____ are legal property rights over creations of the mind, both artistic and commercial, and the corresponding fields of law. Under _____ law, owners are granted certain exclusive rights to a variety of intangible assets, such as musical, literary, and artistic works; ideas, discoveries and inventions; and words, phrases, symbols, and designs. Common types of _____ include copyrights, trademarks, patents, industrial design rights and trade secrets.
   a. ACNielsen
   b. Intellectual Property
   c. Elasticity
   d. Opinion leadership

Chapter 3. E-Commerce and Dispute Resolution

12. _____, a form of alternative dispute resolution (ADR) or 'appropriate dispute resolution', aims to assist two (or more) disputants in reaching an agreement. The parties themselves determine the conditions of any settlements reached-- rather than accepting something imposed by a third party. The disputes may involve (as parties) states, organizations, communities, individuals or other representatives with a vested interest in the outcome.
    a. Specific Performance
    b. Magnuson-Moss Warranty Act
    c. Fair trade law
    d. Mediation

13. _____ is an advertisement in which a particular product specifically mentions a competitor by name for the express purpose of showing why the competitor is inferior to the product naming it.

This should not be confused with parody advertisements, where a fictional product is being advertised for the purpose of poking fun at the particular advertisement, nor should it be confused with the use of a coined brand name for the purpose of comparing the product without actually naming an actual competitor. ('Wikipedia tastes better and is less filling than the Encyclopedia Galactica.')

In the 1980s, during what has been referred to as the cola wars, soft-drink manufacturer Pepsi ran a series of advertisements where people, caught on hidden camera, in a blind taste test, chose Pepsi over rival Coca-Cola.

    a. Heavy-up
    b. GL-70
    c. Comparative advertising
    d. Cost per conversion

14. In some countries, notably the United States, a trademark used to identify a service rather than a product is called a _____ or servicemark. When a _____ is federally registered, the standard registration symbol ® or 'Reg U.S. Pat ' TM Off' may be used (the same symbol is used to mark registered trademarks.) Before it is registered, it is common practice (but has no legal standing) to use the _____ symbol ā„ (a superscript '_____'.)
    a. Screener
    b. Trademark classification
    c. Trespass to land
    d. Service mark

15. A _____ is the name which a business trades under for commercial purposes, although its registered, legal name, used for contracts and other formal situations, may be another. Pharmaceuticals also have _____s, often dissimilar to their chemical names

Trading names are sometimes registered as trademarks or are regarded as brands.

Chapter 3. E-Commerce and Dispute Resolution

a. Local purchasing
b. Niche market
c. Soft currency
d. Trade name

16. _____ is a form of intellectual property which gives the creator of an original work exclusive rights for a certain time period in relation to that work, including its publication, distribution and adaptation; after which time the work is said to enter the public domain. _____ applies to any expressible form of an idea or information that is substantive and discrete. Some jurisdictions also recognize 'moral rights' of the creator of a work, such as the right to be credited for the work.
   a. Celler-Kefauver Act
   b. Reasonable person standard
   c. Collective mark
   d. Copyright

17. A _____ or trade mark, identified by the symbols â„¢ (not yet registered) and Â® (registered) business organization or other legal entity to identify that the products and/or services to consumers with which the _____ appears originate from a unique source of origin, and to distinguish its products or services from those of other entities. A _____ is a type of intellectual property, and typically a name, word, phrase, logo, symbol, design, image, or a combination of these elements. There is also a range of non-conventional _____s comprising marks which do not fall into these standard categories.
   a. 180SearchAssistant
   b. Power III
   c. Risk management
   d. Trademark

18. _____ is a violation of the exclusive rights attaching to a trademark without the authorization of the trademark owner or any licensees (provided that such authorization was within the scope of the license.) Infringement may occur when one party, the 'infringer', uses a trademark which is identical or confusingly similar to a trademark owned by another party, in relation to products or services which are identical or similar to the products or services which the registration covers. An owner of a trademark may commence legal proceedings against a party which infringes its registration.
   a. Trademark classification
   b. Trademark Infringement
   c. Fair Debt Collection Practices Act
   d. Passing off

19. A _____ is a repository usually within the Usenet system, for messages posted from many users in different locations. The term may be confusing to some, because it is usually a discussion group. _____s are technically distinct from, but functionally similar to, discussion forums on the World Wide Web.

a. Power III
b. 180SearchAssistant
c. 6-3-5 Brainwriting
d. Newsgroup

20. _____ is the ability of an individual or group to seclude themselves or information about themselves and thereby reveal themselves selectively. The boundaries and content of what is considered private differ among cultures and individuals, but share basic common themes. _____ is sometimes related to anonymity, the wish to remain unnoticed or unidentified in the public realm.
 a. Power III
 b. 6-3-5 Brainwriting
 c. 180SearchAssistant
 d. Privacy

21. _____ is the practice of individuals including commercial businesses, governments and institutions, facilitating the sale of their products or services to other companies or organizations that in turn resell them, use them as components in products or services they offer _____ is also called business-to-_____ for short. (Note that while marketing to government entities shares some of the same dynamics of organizational marketing, B2G Marketing is meaningfully different.)
 a. Disruptive technology
 b. Mass marketing
 c. Law of disruption
 d. Business marketing

22. _____ is exchange of capital, goods, and services across international borders or territories. In most countries, it represents a significant share of gross domestic product (GDP.) While _____ has been present throughout much of history, its economic, social, and political importance has been on the rise in recent centuries.
 a. ACNielsen
 b. Incoterms
 c. ADTECH
 d. International Trade

Chapter 4. Cyber Torts and Crimes

1. _____ is an American author as well as a practicing lawyer. Turow has written eight fiction and two nonfiction books, which have been translated into over 20 languages and have sold over 25 million copies. Movies have been based on several of his books.
    a. Nouveau riche
    b. Generation X
    c. Scott Turow
    d. Peter Ferdinand Drucker

2. _____ is a fee paid on borrowed assets. It is the price paid for the use of borrowed money, or, money earned by deposited funds. Assets that are sometimes lent with _____ include money, shares, consumer goods through hire purchase, major assets such as aircraft, and even entire factories in finance lease arrangements.
    a. ADTECH
    b. ACNielsen
    c. AMAX
    d. Interest

3. The reasonable person is a legal fiction of the common law representing an objective standard against which any individual's conduct can be measured. It is used to determine if a breach of the standard of care has occurred, provided a duty of care can be proven.

    The _____ holds: each person owes a duty to behave as a reasonable person would under the same or similar circumstances.

    a. Trademark classification
    b. Trade secret
    c. Foreign Corrupt Practices Act
    d. Reasonable person standard

4. In law, _____ also called calumny, libel for written words, slander for spoken words, is the communication of a statement that makes a claim, expressly stated or implied to be factual, that may give an individual, business, product, group, government or nation a negative image. It is usually, but not always, a requirement that this claim be false and that the publication is communicated to someone other than the person defamed

    In common law jurisdictions, slander refers to a malicious, false and defamatory spoken statement or report, while libel refers to any other form of communication such as written words or images.

Chapter 4. Cyber Torts and Crimes

a. Muckraker
b. Free good
c. Free trade zone
d. Defamation

5. _____s function as professionals who deal with trade, dealing in commodities that they do not produce themselves, in order to produce profit.

_____s can be of two types:

1. A wholesale _____ operates in the chain between producer and retail _____. Some wholesale _____s only organize the movement of goods rather than move the goods themselves.
2. A retail _____ or retailer, sells commodities to consumers (including businesses.) A shop owner is a retail _____.

A _____ class characterizes many pre-modern societies. Its status can range from high (even achieving titles like that of _____ prince or nabob) to low, such as in Chinese culture, due to the soiling capabilities of profiting from 'mere' trade, rather than from the labor of others reflected in agricultural produce, craftsmanship, and tribute.

In the United States, '_____' is defined (under the Uniform Commercial Code) as any person while engaged in a business or profession or a seller who deals regularly in the type of goods sold.

a. RFM
b. Trade credit
c. Retail loss prevention
d. Merchant

6. A _____ is a court order issued by a judge or magistrate that authorizes law enforcement to conduct a search of a person or location for evidence of a criminal offense and seize such items. All jurisdictions with a rule of law and a right to privacy put constraints on the powers of police investigators, and typically require _____s, or an equivalent procedure, for searches within a criminal enquiry. There typically also exist exemptions for 'hot pursuit': if a criminal flees the scene of a crime and the police officer follows him, the officer has the right to enter an edifice in which the criminal has sought shelter.

a. 180SearchAssistant
b. Power III
c. 6-3-5 Brainwriting
d. Search warrant

Chapter 4. Cyber Torts and Crimes

7. _____ in United States law is a condition required to establish libel against public officials or public figures and is defined as 'knowledge that the information was false' or that it was published 'with reckless disregard of whether it was false or not.' Reckless disregard does not encompass mere neglect in following professional standards of fact checking. The publisher must entertain actual doubt as to the statement's truth. This is the definition in only the United States and came from the landmark 1964 lawsuit New York Times Co. v. Sullivan, which ruled that public officials needed to prove _____ in order to recover damages for libel.
   a. ADTECH
   b. Actual malice
   c. ACNielsen
   d. AMAX

8. _____ is the area of law concerned with the protection and preservation of the privacy rights of individuals. Increasingly, governments and other public as well as private organizations collect vast amounts of personal information about individuals for a variety of purposes. The law of privacy regulates the type of information which may be collected and how this information may be used.
   a. Collective mark
   b. Madrid system
   c. Trademark attorney
   d. Privacy law

9. _____ is the ability of an individual or group to seclude themselves or information about themselves and thereby reveal themselves selectively. The boundaries and content of what is considered private differ among cultures and individuals, but share basic common themes. _____ is sometimes related to anonymity, the wish to remain unnoticed or unidentified in the public realm.
   a. Privacy
   b. 180SearchAssistant
   c. 6-3-5 Brainwriting
   d. Power III

10. _____ is a form of intellectual property which gives the creator of an original work exclusive rights for a certain time period in relation to that work, including its publication, distribution and adaptation; after which time the work is said to enter the public domain. _____ applies to any expressible form of an idea or information that is substantive and discrete. Some jurisdictions also recognize 'moral rights' of the creator of a work, such as the right to be credited for the work.
   a. Collective mark
   b. Reasonable person standard
   c. Celler-Kefauver Act
   d. Copyright

Chapter 4. Cyber Torts and Crimes

11. _____ is a term commonly used to describe commerce transactions between businesses like the one between a manufacturer and a wholesaler or a wholesaler and a retailer i.e both the buyer and the seller are business entity.This is unlike business-to-consumers (B2C) which involve a business entity and end consumer, or business-to-government (B2G) which involve a business entity and government.

The volume of B2B transactions is much higher than the volume of B2C transactions. The primary reason for this is that in a typical supply chain there will be many B2B transactions involving subcomponent or raw materials, and only one B2C transaction, specifically sale of the finished product to the end customer.

   a. Disruptive technology
   b. Social marketing
   c. Customer relationship management
   d. Business-to-business

12. _____ is a sub-discipline and type of marketing. There are two main definitional characteristics which distinguish it from other types of marketing. The first is that it attempts to send its messages directly to consumers, without the use of intervening media.
   a. Power III
   b. Direct Marketing Associations
   c. Database marketing
   d. Direct Marketing

13. _____ are national trade organizations that seek to advance all forms of direct marketing.

23 direct marketing trade associations from five continents established an International Federation of _____. Founded in 1989, the IFDirect Marketing Associations was established to develop firm lines of communications between direct marketers around the world, and is dedicated to improving the practice and communicating the value of direct marketing; and to promoting the highest standards for ethical conduct and effective self-regulation of the direct marketing community.

   a. Power III
   b. Database marketing
   c. Direct Marketing Associations
   d. Direct marketing

14. _____ is defined by the American _____ Association as the activity, set of institutions, and processes for creating, communicating, delivering, and exchanging offerings that have value for customers, clients, partners, and society at large. The term developed from the original meaning which referred literally to going to market, as in shopping, or going to a market to sell goods or services.

_____ practice tends to be seen as a creative industry, which includes advertising, distribution and selling.

a. Product naming
b. Customer acquisition management
c. Marketing myopia
d. Marketing

15. _____ as a legal term refers to promotional statements and claims that express subjective rather than objective views, such that no reasonable person would take literally. _____ is especially featured in testimonials.

In a legal context, the term originated in the English Court of Appeal case Carlill v Carbolic Smoke Ball Company, which centred on whether a monetary reimbursement should be paid when an influenza preventative device failed to work.

a. Conquesting
b. Heinz pickle pin
c. Custom media
d. Puffery

16. _____, a form of alternative dispute resolution (ADR), is a legal technique for the resolution of disputes outside the courts, wherein the parties to a dispute refer it to one or more persons (the 'arbitrators', 'arbiters' or 'arbitral tribunal'), by whose decision (the 'award') they agree to be bound. It is a settlement technique in which a third party reviews the case and imposes a decision that is legally binding for both sides. Other forms of ADR include mediation (a form of settlement negotiation facilitated by a neutral third party) and non-binding resolution by experts.

a. ADTECH
b. Arbitration
c. AMAX
d. ACNielsen

17. The most important feature of a contract is that one party makes an _____ for an arrangement that another accepts. This can be called a 'concurrence of wills' or 'ad idem' (meeting of the minds) of two or more parties. The concept is somewhat contested.

a. ACNielsen
b. Offer
c. AMAX
d. ADTECH

Chapter 4. Cyber Torts and Crimes

18. Competitiveness is a comparative concept of the ability and performance of a firm, sub-sector or country to sell and supply goods and/or services in a given market. Although widely used in economics and business management, the usefulness of the concept, particularly in the context of national competitiveness, is vigorously disputed by economists, such as Paul Krugman .

The term may also be applied to markets, where it is used to refer to the extent to which the market structure may be regarded as perfectly _____.

   a. Free trade zone
   b. Customs union
   c. Geographical pricing
   d. Competitive

19. _____ is the practice of selling a product or service at a very low price, intending to drive competitors out of the market, or create barriers to entry for potential new competitors. If competitors or potential competitors cannot sustain equal or lower prices without losing money, they go out of business or choose not to enter the business. The predatory merchant then has fewer competitors or is even a de facto monopoly, and can then raise prices above what the market would otherwise bear.
   a. Power III
   b. 180SearchAssistant
   c. List price
   d. Predatory pricing

20. In the common law, _____ refers to one of the three main classes of property, the other two classes being personal property and intellectual property. _____ generally encompasses land, land improvements resulting from human effort including buildings and machinery sited on land, and various property rights over the preceding.

The concept is variously named and defined in other jurisdictions: heritable property in Scotland, immobilier in France, and immovable property in Canada, United States, India, Pakistan, Bangladesh, Malta, Cyprus, and in countries where civil law systems prevail, including most of Europe, Russia, and South America.

   a. Trade secret
   b. Copyright infringement
   c. Real property
   d. Madrid system

21. _____ is a common law tort that is committed when an individual or the object of an individual intentionally (or in Australia negligently) enters the land of another without a lawful excuse. _____ is actionable per se. Thus, the party whose land is entered upon may sue even if no actual harm is done.

a. Sound trademark
b. Madrid system
c. Right to Financial Privacy Act
d. Trespass to land

22. _____ are legal property rights over creations of the mind, both artistic and commercial, and the corresponding fields of law. Under _____ law, owners are granted certain exclusive rights to a variety of intangible assets, such as musical, literary, and artistic works; ideas, discoveries and inventions; and words, phrases, symbols, and designs. Common types of _____ include copyrights, trademarks, patents, industrial design rights and trade secrets.

a. ACNielsen
b. Opinion leadership
c. Intellectual Property
d. Elasticity

23. _____ is a concept that denotes the precise probability of specific eventualities. Technically, the notion of _____ is independent from the notion of value and, as such, eventualities may have both beneficial and adverse consequences. However, in general usage the convention is to focus only on potential negative impact to some characteristic of value that may arise from a future event.

a. Power III
b. 6-3-5 Brainwriting
c. Risk
d. 180SearchAssistant

24. In grammar, the _____ is the form of an adjective or adverb which denotes the degree or grade by which a person, thing and is used in this context with a subordinating conjunction, such as than, as...as, etc.

The structure of a _____ in English consists normally of the positive form of the adjective or adverb, plus the suffix -er e.g. 'he is taller than his father is', or 'the village is less picturesque than the town nearby'.

a. Power III
b. 6-3-5 Brainwriting
c. 180SearchAssistant
d. Comparative

25. _____ is a partial legal defense that reduces the amount of damages that a plaintiff can recover in a negligence-based claim based upon the degree to which the plaintiff's own negligence contributed to cause the injury. When the defense is asserted, the fact-finder, usually a jury, must decide the degree to which the plaintiff's negligence versus the combined negligence of all other relevant actors contributed to cause the plaintiff's damages. It is a modification of the doctrine of contributory negligence which disallows any recovery by a plaintiff whose negligence contributed, even minimally, to causing the damages.
   a. Copyright infringement
   b. Contributory negligence
   c. Registered trademark symbol
   d. Comparative negligence

26. _____ is a common law defense to a claim based on negligence, an action in tort. It applies to cases where a plaintiff has, through his own negligence, contributed to the harm he suffered. For example, a pedestrian crosses a road negligently and is hit by a driver who was driving negligently.
   a. Right to Financial Privacy Act
   b. Country of origin
   c. Contributory negligence
   d. Tenth Amendment

27. _____ is the area of law in which manufacturers, distributors, suppliers, retailers, and others who make products available to the public are held responsible for the injuries those products cause.

In the United States, the claims most commonly associated with _____ are negligence, strict liability, breach of warranty, and various consumer protection claims. The majority of _____ laws are determined at the state level and vary widely from state to state.

   a. Registered trademark symbol
   b. Product liability
   c. Mediation
   d. Trespass to land

28. _____ makes a person responsible for the damage and loss caused by his/her acts and omissions regardless of culpability .) _____ is important in torts (especially product liability), corporations law, and criminal law. For analysis of the pros and cons of _____ as applied to product liability, the most important _____ regime, see product liability.
   a. Maturity of Organizations and Business Excellence - The Four-Phase Model
   b. Consumption Map
   c. Strict liability
   d. Black PRies

Chapter 4. Cyber Torts and Crimes

29. _____ is the unauthorized use of material that is covered by copyright law, in a manner that violates one of the copyright owner's exclusive rights, such as the right to reproduce or perform the copyrighted work, or to make derivative works.

For electronic and audio-visual media, unauthorized reproduction and distribution is occasionally referred to as piracy . The practice of labeling the act of infringement as 'piracy' actually predates copyright itself.

   a. Non-conventional trademark
   b. Copyright infringement
   c. Mediation
   d. Patent

30. _____ is an advertisement in which a particular product specifically mentions a competitor by name for the express purpose of showing why the competitor is inferior to the product naming it.

This should not be confused with parody advertisements, where a fictional product is being advertised for the purpose of poking fun at the particular advertisement, nor should it be confused with the use of a coined brand name for the purpose of comparing the product without actually naming an actual competitor. ('Wikipedia tastes better and is less filling than the Encyclopedia Galactica.')

In the 1980s, during what has been referred to as the cola wars, soft-drink manufacturer Pepsi ran a series of advertisements where people, caught on hidden camera, in a blind taste test, chose Pepsi over rival Coca-Cola.

   a. Heavy-up
   b. GL-70
   c. Cost per conversion
   d. Comparative advertising

31. A _____ is an entity that provides services to other entities. Usually this refers to a business that provides subscription or web service to other businesses or individuals. Examples of these services include Internet access, Mobile phone operator, and web application hosting.
   a. Cross-selling
   b. Yield management
   c. Service provider
   d. Freebie marketing

32. _____ is a broad label that refers to any individuals or households that use goods and services generated within the economy. The concept of a _____ is used in different contexts, so that the usage and significance of the term may vary.

Chapter 4. Cyber Torts and Crimes

A _____ is a person who uses any product or service.

a. Power III
b. Consumer
c. 6-3-5 Brainwriting
d. 180SearchAssistant

33. _____ is a form of government regulation which protects the interests of consumers. For example, a government may require businesses to disclose detailed information about products--particularly in areas where safety or public health is an issue, such as food. _____ is linked to the idea of consumer rights (that consumers have various rights as consumers), and to the formation of consumer organizations which help consumers make better choices in the marketplace.

a. Trademark dilution
b. Federal Bureau of Investigation
c. Sound trademark
d. Consumer Protection

34. _____, commonly known as e-commerce or eCommerce, consists of the buying and selling of products or services over electronic systems such as the Internet and other computer networks. The amount of trade conducted electronically has grown extraordinarily with wide-spread Internet usage. A wide variety of commerce is conducted in this way, spurring and drawing on innovations in electronic funds transfer, supply chain management, Internet marketing, online transaction processing, electronic data interchange (EDI), inventory management systems, and automated data collection systems.

a. Electronic Commerce
b. AMAX
c. ACNielsen
d. ADTECH

35. _____, cybercrime, e-crime, hi-tech crime or electronic crime generally refers to criminal activity where a computer or network is the source, tool, target, or place of a crime. These categories are not exclusive and many activities can be characterized as falling in one or more. Additionally, although the terms _____ and cybercrime are more properly restricted to describing criminal activity in which the computer or network is a necessary part of the crime, these terms are also sometimes used to include traditional crimes, such as fraud, theft, blackmail, forgery, and embezzlement, in which computers or networks are used.

a. Computer crime
b. Power III
c. 6-3-5 Brainwriting
d. 180SearchAssistant

Chapter 4. Cyber Torts and Crimes

36. In the technical language of the World Trade Organization (WTO) system, a _____ is used to restrain international trade in order to protect a certain home industry from foreign competition. A member may take a '_____' action (i.e., restrict importation of a product temporarily) to protect a specific domestic industry from an increase in imports of any product which is causing, or which is threatening to cause, serious injury to the domestic industry that produces like or directly-competitive products.

_____ measures were always available under the General Agreement on Tariffs and Trade (GATT) (Article XIX).

   a. Countervailing duties
   b. Customs union
   c. Gray market
   d. Safeguard

37. _____ is a statistical phenomenon in marketing where, with few exceptions, brand loyalty is lower among buyers of low market share brands than buyers of high market share brands. The market leader in an industry enjoys a high level of sales due to customer loyalty, with a higher probability of repeat purchase. This phenomenon occurs because consumers believe the high sales product to be of high quality.
   a. 6-3-5 Brainwriting
   b. 180SearchAssistant
   c. Power III
   d. Double jeopardy

38. A _____ product is an imitation which infringes upon a production monopoly held by either a state or corporation. Goods are produced with the intent to bypass this monopoly and thus take advantage of the established worth of the previous product. The word _____ frequently describes both the forgeries of currency and documents, as well as the imitations of clothing, software, pharmaceuticals, watches, electronics, and company logos and brands.
   a. 6-3-5 Brainwriting
   b. 180SearchAssistant
   c. Power III
   d. Counterfeit

39. The _____ is a very large set of interlinked hypertext documents accessed via the Internet. With a Web browser, one can view Web pages that may contain text, images, videos, and other multimedia and navigate between them using hyperlinks. Using concepts from earlier hypertext systems, the _____ was begun in 1992 by the English physicist Sir Tim Berners-Lee, now the Director of the _____ Consortium, and Robert Cailliau, a Belgian computer scientist, while both were working at CERN in Geneva, Switzerland.

a. 180SearchAssistant
b. Power III
c. 6-3-5 Brainwriting
d. World Wide Web

40. A _____ or trade mark, identified by the symbols â"¢ (not yet registered) and Â® (registered) business organization or other legal entity to identify that the products and/or services to consumers with which the _____ appears originate from a unique source of origin, and to distinguish its products or services from those of other entities. A _____ is a type of intellectual property, and typically a name, word, phrase, logo, symbol, design, image, or a combination of these elements. There is also a range of non-conventional _____s comprising marks which do not fall into these standard categories.
    a. Power III
    b. Trademark
    c. Risk management
    d. 180SearchAssistant

41. The _____ is the primary unit in the United States Department of Justice, serving as both a federal criminal investigative body and a domestic intelligence agency. The FBI has investigative jurisdiction over violations of more than 200 categories of federal crime. Its motto is 'Fidelity, Bravery, Integrity,' corresponding to the 'FBI' initialism.
    a. Federal Bureau of Investigation
    b. Foreign Corrupt Practices Act
    c. Trademark dilution
    d. Service mark

Chapter 5. Intellectual Property—Patents and Copyrights

1. _____ is a form of intellectual property which gives the creator of an original work exclusive rights for a certain time period in relation to that work, including its publication, distribution and adaptation; after which time the work is said to enter the public domain. _____ applies to any expressible form of an idea or information that is substantive and discrete. Some jurisdictions also recognize 'moral rights' of the creator of a work, such as the right to be credited for the work.
    a. Copyright
    b. Celler-Kefauver Act
    c. Reasonable person standard
    d. Collective mark

2. _____ are legal property rights over creations of the mind, both artistic and commercial, and the corresponding fields of law. Under _____ law, owners are granted certain exclusive rights to a variety of intangible assets, such as musical, literary, and artistic works; ideas, discoveries and inventions; and words, phrases, symbols, and designs. Common types of _____ include copyrights, trademarks, patents, industrial design rights and trade secrets.
    a. Elasticity
    b. ACNielsen
    c. Opinion leadership
    d. Intellectual property

3. A _____ is a set of exclusive rights granted by a State to an inventor or his assignee for a limited period of time in exchange for a disclosure of an invention.

    The procedure for granting _____s, the requirements placed on the _____ee and the extent of the exclusive rights vary widely between countries according to national laws and international agreements. Typically, however, a _____ application must include one or more claims defining the invention which must be new, inventive, and useful or industrially applicable.

    a. Foreign Corrupt Practices Act
    b. Product liability
    c. Reasonable person standard
    d. Patent

4. _____ is an advertisement in which a particular product specifically mentions a competitor by name for the express purpose of showing why the competitor is inferior to the product naming it.

    This should not be confused with parody advertisements, where a fictional product is being advertised for the purpose of poking fun at the particular advertisement, nor should it be confused with the use of a coined brand name for the purpose of comparing the product without actually naming an actual competitor. ('Wikipedia tastes better and is less filling than the Encyclopedia Galactica.')

    In the 1980s, during what has been referred to as the cola wars, soft-drink manufacturer Pepsi ran a series of advertisements where people, caught on hidden camera, in a blind taste test, chose Pepsi over rival Coca-Cola.

Chapter 5. Intellectual Property—Patents and Copyrights

a. Cost per conversion
b. GL-70
c. Heavy-up
d. Comparative advertising

5. In some countries, notably the United States, a trademark used to identify a service rather than a product is called a _____ or servicemark. When a _____ is federally registered, the standard registration symbol ® or 'Reg U.S. Pat ' TM Off' may be used (the same symbol is used to mark registered trademarks.) Before it is registered, it is common practice (but has no legal standing) to use the _____ symbol ā„ (a superscript '_____'.)

   a. Service mark
   b. Screener
   c. Trespass to land
   d. Trademark classification

6. A _____ is a formula, practice, process, design, instrument, pattern by which a business can obtain an economic advantage over competitors or customers. In some jurisdictions, such secrets are referred to as 'confidential information' or 'classified information'.

   The precise language by which a _____ is defined varies by jurisdiction (as do the particular types of information that are subject to _____ protection.)

   a. Federal Bureau of Investigation
   b. CAN-SPAM
   c. Trade secret
   d. Priority right

7. A _____ or trade mark, identified by the symbols ā„¢ (not yet registered) and ® (registered) business organization or other legal entity to identify that the products and/or services to consumers with which the _____ appears originate from a unique source of origin, and to distinguish its products or services from those of other entities. A _____ is a type of intellectual property, and typically a name, word, phrase, logo, symbol, design, image, or a combination of these elements. There is also a range of non-conventional _____ s comprising marks which do not fall into these standard categories.

   a. Power III
   b. Risk management
   c. 180SearchAssistant
   d. Trademark

Chapter 5. Intellectual Property—Patents and Copyrights

8. _____ is a legal term of art that generally refers to characteristics of the visual appearance of a product or its packaging (or even the design of a building) that signify the source of the product to consumers. _____ is a form of intellectual property. In the U.S., like trademarks, a product's _____ is legally protected by the Lanham Act, the federal statute which regulates trademarks and _____.

   a. Trade dress
   b. Gripe site
   c. Wheeler-Lea Act
   d. Geographical indication

9. The _____ is an agency in the United States Department of Commerce that issues patents to inventors and businesses for their inventions, and trademark registration for product and intellectual property identification.

The USPTO is currently based in Alexandria, Virginia, after a 2006 move from the Crystal City area of Arlington, Virginia. The offices under Patents and the Chief Information Officer that remained just outside the southern end of Crystal City completed moving to Randolph Square, a brand new building in Shirlington Village, on 27 April 2009.

   a. INVISTA
   b. Underwriters Laboratories
   c. United States Patent and Trademark Office
   d. Access Commerce

10. The _____ is a very large set of interlinked hypertext documents accessed via the Internet. With a Web browser, one can view Web pages that may contain text, images, videos, and other multimedia and navigate between them using hyperlinks. Using concepts from earlier hypertext systems, the _____ was begun in 1992 by the English physicist Sir Tim Berners-Lee, now the Director of the _____ Consortium, and Robert Cailliau, a Belgian computer scientist, while both were working at CERN in Geneva, Switzerland.

   a. Power III
   b. 6-3-5 Brainwriting
   c. World Wide Web
   d. 180SearchAssistant

11. A _____ is a structured collection of records or data that is stored in a computer system. The structure is achieved by organizing the data according to a _____ model. The model in most common use today is the relational model.

   a. 6-3-5 Brainwriting
   b. Power III
   c. 180SearchAssistant
   d. Database

Chapter 5. Intellectual Property—Patents and Copyrights

12. _____ is the unauthorized use of material that is covered by copyright law, in a manner that violates one of the copyright owner's exclusive rights, such as the right to reproduce or perform the copyrighted work, or to make derivative works.

For electronic and audio-visual media, unauthorized reproduction and distribution is occasionally referred to as piracy . The practice of labeling the act of infringement as 'piracy' actually predates copyright itself.

   a. Mediation
   b. Non-conventional trademark
   c. Patent
   d. Copyright infringement

13. _____ is a doctrine in United States copyright law that allows limited use of copyrighted material without requiring permission from the rights holders, such as use for scholarship or review. It provides for the legal, non-licensed citation or incorporation of copyrighted material in another author's work under a four-factor balancing test. The term '_____' originated in the United States, but has been added to Israeli law as well; a similar principle, fair dealing, exists in some other common law jurisdictions.
   a. AStore
   b. F. Lee Bailey
   c. African Americans
   d. Fair use

14. _____ is a broad label that refers to any individuals or households that use goods and services generated within the economy. The concept of a _____ is used in different contexts, so that the usage and significance of the term may vary.

A _____ is a person who uses any product or service.

   a. 180SearchAssistant
   b. Consumer
   c. Power III
   d. 6-3-5 Brainwriting

15. _____ is a form of government regulation which protects the interests of consumers. For example, a government may require businesses to disclose detailed information about products--particularly in areas where safety or public health is an issue, such as food. _____ is linked to the idea of consumer rights (that consumers have various rights as consumers), and to the formation of consumer organizations which help consumers make better choices in the marketplace.

a. Consumer Protection
b. Federal Bureau of Investigation
c. Sound trademark
d. Trademark dilution

16. _____, commonly known as e-commerce or eCommerce, consists of the buying and selling of products or services over electronic systems such as the Internet and other computer networks. The amount of trade conducted electronically has grown extraordinarily with wide-spread Internet usage. A wide variety of commerce is conducted in this way, spurring and drawing on innovations in electronic funds transfer, supply chain management, Internet marketing, online transaction processing, electronic data interchange (EDI), inventory management systems, and automated data collection systems.
    a. ADTECH
    b. AMAX
    c. ACNielsen
    d. Electronic Commerce

17. An _____ is the manufacturing of a good or service within a category. Although _____ is a broad term for any kind of economic production, in economics and urban planning _____ is a synonym for the secondary sector, which is a type of economic activity involved in the manufacturing of raw materials into goods and products.

There are four key industrial economic sectors: the primary sector, largely raw material extraction industries such as mining and farming; the secondary sector, involving refining, construction, and manufacturing; the tertiary sector, which deals with services (such as law and medicine) and distribution of manufactured goods; and the quaternary sector, a relatively new type of knowledge _____ focusing on technological research, design and development such as computer programming, and biochemistry.

   a. AMAX
   b. ADTECH
   c. Industry
   d. ACNielsen

18. In cryptography, _____ is the process of transforming information (referred to as plaintext) using an algorithm (called cipher) to make it unreadable to anyone except those possessing special knowledge, usually referred to as a key. The result of the process is encrypted information (in cryptography, referred to as ciphertext.) In many contexts, the word _____ also implicitly refers to the reverse process, decryption (e.g. 'software for _____' can typically also perform decryption), to make the encrypted information readable again (i.e. to make it unencrypted.)

Chapter 5. Intellectual Property—Patents and Copyrights

a. ADTECH
b. AMAX
c. ACNielsen
d. Encryption

19. The _____ is a United States copyright law that implements two 1996 treaties of the World Intellectual Property Organization (WIPO.) It criminalizes production and dissemination of technology, devices whether or not there is actual infringement of copyright itself. In addition, the _____ heightens the penalties for copyright infringement on the Internet.
   a. Copyright infringement
   b. Priority right
   c. Regulatory
   d. Digital Millennium Copyright Act

20. A _____ is an entity that provides services to other entities. Usually this refers to a business that provides subscription or web service to other businesses or individuals. Examples of these services include Internet access, Mobile phone operator, and web application hosting.
   a. Cross-selling
   b. Yield management
   c. Service provider
   d. Freebie marketing

21. _____ Fox 2000 Pictures is one of the six major American film studios. Located in the Century City area of Los Angeles, just west of Beverly Hills, the studio is a subsidiary of News Corporation, the media conglomerate owned by Rupert Murdoch. The company was founded in 1935, as the result of a merger of two entities, Fox Film Corporation founded by William Fox in 1915, and Twentieth Century Pictures, begun in 1933 by Darryl F. Zanuck, Joseph Schenck, Raymond Griffith and William Goetz.
   a. Power III
   b. Maid in Manhattan
   c. 180SearchAssistant
   d. Twentieth Century Fox Film Corporation

22. _____ networking is a method of delivering computer network services in which the participants share a portion of their own resources, such as processing power, disk storage, network bandwidth, printing facilities. Such resources are provided directly to other participants without intermediary network hosts or servers. _____ network participants are providers and consumers of network services simultaneously, which contrasts with other service models, such as traditional client-server computing.

a. 6-3-5 Brainwriting
b. Power III
c. Peer-to-peer
d. 180SearchAssistant

23. The _____, commonly referred to as HP, is a technology corporation headquartered in Palo Alto, California, United States. HP is the largest technology company in the world and operates in nearly every country. HP specializes in developing and manufacturing computing, storage, and networking hardware, software and services.

a. 180SearchAssistant
b. Hewlett-Packard Company
c. Power III
d. 6-3-5 Brainwriting

24. The _____ is an international agreement administered by the World Trade Organization (WTO) that sets down minimum standards for many forms of intellectual property (IP) regulation. It was negotiated at the end of the Uruguay Round of the General Agreement on Tariffs and Trade (GATT) in 1994.

Specifically, TRIPS contains requirements that nations' laws must meet for: copyright rights, including the rights of performers, producers of sound recordings and broadcasting organizations; geographical indications, including appellations of origin; industrial designs; integrated circuit layout-designs; patents; monopolies for the developers of new plant varieties; trademarks; trade dress; and undisclosed or confidential information.

a. AMAX
b. Agreement on Trade Related Aspects of Intellectual Property Rights
c. ACNielsen
d. ADTECH

25. The _____ is an international organization designed to supervise and liberalize international trade. The _____ came into being on 1 January 1995, and is the successor to the General Agreement on Tariffs and Trade (GATT), which was created in 1947, and continued to operate for almost five decades as a de facto international organization.

The _____ deals with the rules of trade between nations at a near-global level; it is responsible for negotiating and implementing new trade agreements, and is in charge of policing member countries' adherence to all the _____ agreements, signed by the majority of the world's trading nations and ratified in their parliaments.

a. Population Reference Bureau
b. Merchandise Mart
c. World Trade Organization
d. BSI Group

Chapter 6. Intellectual Property—Trademarks, Cyber Marks, and Trade Secrets

1. A _____ or trade mark, identified by the symbols ™ (not yet registered) and ® (registered) business organization or other legal entity to identify that the products and/or services to consumers with which the _____ appears originate from a unique source of origin, and to distinguish its products or services from those of other entities. A _____ is a type of intellectual property, and typically a name, word, phrase, logo, symbol, design, image, or a combination of these elements. There is also a range of non-conventional _____s comprising marks which do not fall into these standard categories.
   a. Power III
   b. Risk management
   c. 180SearchAssistant
   d. Trademark

2. A _____ is a set of exclusive rights granted by a State to an inventor or his assignee for a limited period of time in exchange for a disclosure of an invention.

   The procedure for granting _____s, the requirements placed on the _____ee and the extent of the exclusive rights vary widely between countries according to national laws and international agreements. Typically, however, a _____ application must include one or more claims defining the invention which must be new, inventive, and useful or industrially applicable.

   a. Foreign Corrupt Practices Act
   b. Product liability
   c. Patent
   d. Reasonable person standard

3. _____ is a trademark law concept permitting the owner of a famous trademark to forbid others from using that mark in a way that would lessen its uniqueness. In most cases, _____ involves an unauthorized use of another's trademark on products that do not compete with, and have little connection with, those of the trademark owner. For example, a famous trademark used by one company to refer to hair care products might be diluted if another company began using a similar mark to refer to breakfast cereals or spark plugs.
   a. Trespass to land
   b. Trademark Dilution
   c. Federal Bureau of Investigation
   d. Trademark attorney

4. The _____ is an agency in the United States Department of Commerce that issues patents to inventors and businesses for their inventions, and trademark registration for product and intellectual property identification.

   The USPTO is currently based in Alexandria, Virginia, after a 2006 move from the Crystal City area of Arlington, Virginia. The offices under Patents and the Chief Information Officer that remained just outside the southern end of Crystal City completed moving to Randolph Square, a brand new building in Shirlington Village, on 27 April 2009.

Chapter 6. Intellectual Property—Trademarks, Cyber Marks, and Trade Secrets

a. INVISTA
b. Access Commerce
c. Underwriters Laboratories
d. United States Patent and Trademark Office

5. _____ is the ability of an individual or group to seclude themselves or information about themselves and thereby reveal themselves selectively. The boundaries and content of what is considered private differ among cultures and individuals, but share basic common themes. _____ is sometimes related to anonymity, the wish to remain unnoticed or unidentified in the public realm.
   a. 180SearchAssistant
   b. Power III
   c. 6-3-5 Brainwriting
   d. Privacy

6. _____ is a form of intellectual property which gives the creator of an original work exclusive rights for a certain time period in relation to that work, including its publication, distribution and adaptation; after which time the work is said to enter the public domain. _____ applies to any expressible form of an idea or information that is substantive and discrete. Some jurisdictions also recognize 'moral rights' of the creator of a work, such as the right to be credited for the work.
   a. Celler-Kefauver Act
   b. Collective mark
   c. Reasonable person standard
   d. Copyright

7. Trademark _____ is an important concept in the law governing trademarks and service marks. A trademark may be eligible for registration, or registrable, if amongst other things it performs the essential trademark function, and has distinctive character. Registrability can be understood as a continuum, with 'inherently distinctive' marks at one end, 'generic' and 'descriptive' marks with no distinctive character at the other end, and 'suggestive' and 'arbitrary' marks lying between these two points.
   a. Distinctiveness
   b. Brand implementation
   c. Brand ambassador
   d. Corporate colours

8. _____ is a violation of the exclusive rights attaching to a trademark without the authorization of the trademark owner or any licensees (provided that such authorization was within the scope of the license.) Infringement may occur when one party, the 'infringer', uses a trademark which is identical or confusingly similar to a trademark owned by another party, in relation to products or services which are identical or similar to the products or services which the registration covers. An owner of a trademark may commence legal proceedings against a party which infringes its registration.

Chapter 6. Intellectual Property—Trademarks, Cyber Marks, and Trade Secrets

    a. Passing off
    b. Trademark classification
    c. Fair Debt Collection Practices Act
    d. Trademark Infringement

9. _____ refers to the confirmation of certain characteristics of an object, person, or organization. This confirmation is often, but not always, provided by some form of external review, education, or assessment. One of the most common types of _____ in modern society is professional _____, where a person is certified as being able to competently complete a job or task, usually by the passing of an examination.
    a. Power III
    b. 180SearchAssistant
    c. Certification
    d. 6-3-5 Brainwriting

10. A _____ on a commercial product indicates five things:

- The existence of a legal follow-up or product certification agreement between the manufacturer of a product and an organisation with national accreditation for both testing and certification,
- Legal evidence that the product was successfully tested in accordance with a nationally accredited standard,
- Legal assurance the accredited certification organization has ensured that the item that was successfully tested and is identical to that which is being offered for sale,
- Legal assurance that the successful test has resulted in a certification listing, which is considered public information, which sets out the tolerances and conditions of use for the certified product, to enable compliance with the law through listing and approval use and compliance,
- Legal assurance that the manufacturer is being regularly audited by the certification organisation to ensure the maintenance of the original process standard that was employed in the manufacture of the test specimen that passed the test. If the manufacturer should fail an audit, all product that was certified, including labels of stock on hand, on construction sites, with end-user customers and on distributor store shelves, can be mandated by the cirtification organisation in charge to be immediately removed, and can insist that all stakeholders be informed that the de-listed product certification is no longer eligible for use in field installations.

On the part of the certifier, the label itself is a type of trademark whereby the listee, or manufacturer, uses the mark to indicate eligibility of the products for use in field installations in accordance with the requirements of the code, and/or the origin, material, mode of manufacture of products, mode of performance of services, quality, accuracy of other characteristics of products or services.

_____s differ from collective trade marks. The main difference is that collective trade marks may be used by particular members of the organization which owns them, while _____s are the only evidence of the existence of follow-up agreements between manufacturers and nationally accredited testing and certification organisations. Certification organisations charge for the use of their labels and are thus always aware of exact production numbers.

Chapter 6. Intellectual Property—Trademarks, Cyber Marks, and Trade Secrets

a. Certification mark
b. Recognized Component Mark
c. Conformance mark
d. Kitemark

11. A collective trade mark or _____ is a trademark owned by an organisation (such as an association), whose members use them to identify themselves with a level of quality or accuracy, geographical origin, or other characteristics set by the organisation.

Collective trade marks are exceptions to the underlying principle of trade marks in that most trade marks serve as 'badges of origin' - they indicate the individual source of the goods or services. A collective trade mark, however, can be used by a variety of traders, rather than just one individual concern, provided that the trader belongs to the association.

a. Collective trade mark
b. Trade dress
c. Collective mark
d. Privacy law

12. _____ is an advertisement in which a particular product specifically mentions a competitor by name for the express purpose of showing why the competitor is inferior to the product naming it.

This should not be confused with parody advertisements, where a fictional product is being advertised for the purpose of poking fun at the particular advertisement, nor should it be confused with the use of a coined brand name for the purpose of comparing the product without actually naming an actual competitor. ('Wikipedia tastes better and is less filling than the Encyclopedia Galactica.')

In the 1980s, during what has been referred to as the cola wars, soft-drink manufacturer Pepsi ran a series of advertisements where people, caught on hidden camera, in a blind taste test, chose Pepsi over rival Coca-Cola.

a. GL-70
b. Heavy-up
c. Cost per conversion
d. Comparative advertising

13. In some countries, notably the United States, a trademark used to identify a service rather than a product is called a _____ or servicemark. When a _____ is federally registered, the standard registration symbol ® or 'Reg U.S. Pat ' TM Off' may be used (the same symbol is used to mark registered trademarks.) Before it is registered, it is common practice (but has no legal standing) to use the _____ symbol ā„ (a superscript '_____'.)

Chapter 6. Intellectual Property—Trademarks, Cyber Marks, and Trade Secrets

a. Screener
b. Trademark classification
c. Trespass to land
d. Service mark

14. _____ is a legal term of art that generally refers to characteristics of the visual appearance of a product or its packaging (or even the design of a building) that signify the source of the product to consumers. _____ is a form of intellectual property. In the U.S., like trademarks, a product's _____ is legally protected by the Lanham Act, the federal statute which regulates trademarks and _____.

a. Gripe site
b. Wheeler-Lea Act
c. Geographical indication
d. Trade dress

15. A _____ is the name which a business trades under for commercial purposes, although its registered, legal name, used for contracts and other formal situations, may be another. Pharmaceuticals also have _____s, often dissimilar to their chemical names

Trading names are sometimes registered as trademarks or are regarded as brands.

a. Soft currency
b. Local purchasing
c. Niche market
d. Trade name

16. _____ is a broad label that refers to any individuals or households that use goods and services generated within the economy. The concept of a _____ is used in different contexts, so that the usage and significance of the term may vary.

A _____ is a person who uses any product or service.

a. 180SearchAssistant
b. 6-3-5 Brainwriting
c. Power III
d. Consumer

Chapter 6. Intellectual Property—Trademarks, Cyber Marks, and Trade Secrets

17. _____, according to the United States federal law known as the Anticybersquatting Consumer Protection Act, is registering, trafficking in, or using a domain name with bad faith intent to profit from the goodwill of a trademark belonging to someone else. The cybersquatter then offers to sell the domain to the person or company who owns a trademark contained within the name at an inflated price.

The term is derived from 'squatting,' which is the act of occupying an abandoned or unoccupied space or building that the squatter does not own, rent or otherwise have permission to use.

   a. Wildcard DNS record
   b. Domain name warehousing
   c. Fast flux
   d. Cybersquatting

18. A _____ or domain name (TLD) is the highest level of domain names in the root zone of the Domain Name System of the Internet. For all domains in lower levels, it is the last part of the domain name, that is, the label that follows the last dot of a fully qualified domain name. For example, in the domain name `www.example.com`, the _____ is `com` (or `COM`, as domain names are not case-sensitive.)

   a. Top-level domain
   b. Domain name speculation
   c. Typosquatting
   d. Domain name drop list

19. Electronic commerce, commonly known as _____ or eCommerce, consists of the buying and selling of products or services over electronic systems such as the Internet and other computer networks. The amount of trade conducted electronically has grown extraordinarily with wide-spread Internet usage. A wide variety of commerce is conducted in this way, spurring and drawing on innovations in electronic funds transfer, supply chain management, Internet marketing, online transaction processing, electronic data interchange (EDI), inventory management systems, and automated data collection systems.

   a. ADTECH
   b. E-commerce
   c. AMAX
   d. ACNielsen

20. The United States _____ is the Cabinet department of the United States government concerned with promoting economic growth. It was originally created as the United States _____ and Labor on February 14, 1903. It was subsequently renamed to the _____ on March 4, 1913, and its bureaus and agencies specializing in labor were transferred to the new Department of Labor.

Chapter 6. Intellectual Property—Trademarks, Cyber Marks, and Trade Secrets

a. Power III
b. 180SearchAssistant
c. 6-3-5 Brainwriting
d. Department of Commerce

21. The _____ is the Cabinet department of the United States government concerned with promoting economic growth. It was originally created as the _____ and Labor on February 14, 1903. It was subsequently renamed to the Department of Commerce on March 4, 1913, and its bureaus and agencies specializing in labor were transferred to the new Department of Labor.
    a. ACNielsen
    b. ADTECH
    c. AMAX
    d. United States Department of Commerce

22. The _____ is a very large set of interlinked hypertext documents accessed via the Internet. With a Web browser, one can view Web pages that may contain text, images, videos, and other multimedia and navigate between them using hyperlinks. Using concepts from earlier hypertext systems, the _____ was begun in 1992 by the English physicist Sir Tim Berners-Lee, now the Director of the _____ Consortium, and Robert Cailliau, a Belgian computer scientist, while both were working at CERN in Geneva, Switzerland.
    a. 6-3-5 Brainwriting
    b. Power III
    c. 180SearchAssistant
    d. World Wide Web

23. _____ is a term commonly used to describe commerce transactions between businesses like the one between a manufacturer and a wholesaler or a wholesaler and a retailer i.e both the buyer and the seller are business entity. This is unlike business-to-consumers (B2C) which involve a business entity and end consumer, or business-to-government (B2G) which involve a business entity and government.

The volume of B2B transactions is much higher than the volume of B2C transactions. The primary reason for this is that in a typical supply chain there will be many B2B transactions involving subcomponent or raw materials, and only one B2C transaction, specifically sale of the finished product to the end customer.

   a. Social marketing
   b. Business-to-business
   c. Customer relationship management
   d. Disruptive technology

Chapter 6. Intellectual Property—Trademarks, Cyber Marks, and Trade Secrets

24. The verb _____ or grant _____ means to give permission. The noun _____ refers to that permission as well as to the document memorializing that permission. _____ may be granted by a party to another party as an element of an agreement between those parties.
    a. License
    b. 180SearchAssistant
    c. Power III
    d. 6-3-5 Brainwriting

25. _____ is anything that is generally accepted as payment for goods and services and repayment of debts. The main uses of _____ are as a medium of exchange, a unit of account, and a store of value. Some authors explicitly require _____ to be a standard of deferred payment.
    a. Leading indicator
    b. Law of supply
    c. Microeconomics
    d. Money

26. A _____ is a formula, practice, process, design, instrument, pattern by which a business can obtain an economic advantage over competitors or customers. In some jurisdictions, such secrets are referred to as 'confidential information' or 'classified information'.

    The precise language by which a _____ is defined varies by jurisdiction (as do the particular types of information that are subject to _____ protection.)

    a. Trade Secret
    b. Priority right
    c. Federal Bureau of Investigation
    d. CAN-SPAM

27. The _____ is a model law drafted by the National Conference of Commissioners on Uniform State Laws to better define rights and remedies of common law trade secret. It has been adopted by 46 states, the District of Columbia and the U.S. Virgin Islands. Massachusetts, New Jersey, New York and Texas have not adopted the _____.
    a. ADTECH
    b. ACNielsen
    c. Uniform Trade Secrets Act
    d. AMAX

Chapter 6. Intellectual Property—Trademarks, Cyber Marks, and Trade Secrets

28. _____ is a rivalry between individuals, groups, nations for territory, a niche, or allocation of resources. It arises whenever two or more parties strive for a goal which cannot be shared. _____ occurs naturally between living organisms which co-exist in the same environment.
   a. Price fixing
   b. Price competition
   c. Competition
   d. Non-price competition

29. A non-compete clause or _____, is a term used in contract law under which one party (usually an employee) agrees to not pursue a similar profession or trade in competition against another party (usually the employer.) As a contract provision, a CNC is bound by traditional contract requirements including the consideration doctrine. The use of such clauses is premised on the possibility that upon their termination or resignation, an employee might begin working for a competitor or starting a business, and gain competitive advantage by abusing confidential information about their former employer's operations or trade secrets, or sensitive information such as customer/client lists, business practices, upcoming products, and marketing plans.
   a. Hologram trademark
   b. Covenant not to compete
   c. Right to Financial Privacy Act
   d. Copyright

Chapter 7. Online Marketing

1. _____, also referred to as i-marketing, web marketing, online marketing is the marketing of products or services over the Internet.

The Internet has brought many unique benefits to marketing, one of which being lower costs for the distribution of information and media to a global audience. The interactive nature of _____, both in terms of providing instant response and eliciting responses, is a unique quality of the medium.

   a. AMAX
   b. ADTECH
   c. Internet marketing
   d. ACNielsen

2. _____ was an American author, poet, naturalist, tax resister, development critic, surveyor, historian, philosopher, and leading transcendentalist. He is best known for his book Walden, a reflection upon simple living in natural surroundings, and his essay, Civil Disobedience, an argument for individual resistance to civil government in moral opposition to an unjust state.

Thoreau's books, articles, essays, journals, and poetry total over 20 volumes.

   a. AStore
   b. Henry David Thoreau
   c. Albert Einstein
   d. African Americans

3. _____ is defined by the American _____ Association as the activity, set of institutions, and processes for creating, communicating, delivering, and exchanging offerings that have value for customers, clients, partners, and society at large. The term developed from the original meaning which referred literally to going to market, as in shopping, or going to a market to sell goods or services.

_____ practice tends to be seen as a creative industry, which includes advertising, distribution and selling.

   a. Marketing
   b. Marketing myopia
   c. Product naming
   d. Customer acquisition management

4. _____ is a term commonly used to describe commerce transactions between businesses like the one between a manufacturer and a wholesaler or a wholesaler and a retailer i.e both the buyer and the seller are business entity. This is unlike business-to-consumers (B2C) which involve a business entity and end consumer, or business-to-government (B2G) which involve a business entity and government.

50   *Chapter 7. Online Marketing*

The volume of B2B transactions is much higher than the volume of B2C transactions. The primary reason for this is that in a typical supply chain there will be many B2B transactions involving subcomponent or raw materials, and only one B2C transaction, specifically sale of the finished product to the end customer.

   a. Disruptive technology
   b. Customer relationship management
   c. Social marketing
   d. Business-to-business

5. The _____ is a very large set of interlinked hypertext documents accessed via the Internet. With a Web browser, one can view Web pages that may contain text, images, videos, and other multimedia and navigate between them using hyperlinks. Using concepts from earlier hypertext systems, the _____ was begun in 1992 by the English physicist Sir Tim Berners-Lee, now the Director of the _____ Consortium, and Robert Cailliau, a Belgian computer scientist, while both were working at CERN in Geneva, Switzerland.
   a. World Wide Web
   b. 180SearchAssistant
   c. 6-3-5 Brainwriting
   d. Power III

6. _____ is a form of intellectual property which gives the creator of an original work exclusive rights for a certain time period in relation to that work, including its publication, distribution and adaptation; after which time the work is said to enter the public domain. _____ applies to any expressible form of an idea or information that is substantive and discrete. Some jurisdictions also recognize 'moral rights' of the creator of a work, such as the right to be credited for the work.
   a. Collective mark
   b. Copyright
   c. Celler-Kefauver Act
   d. Reasonable person standard

7. A _____ or trade mark, identified by the symbols ™ (not yet registered) and ® (registered) business organization or other legal entity to identify that the products and/or services to consumers with which the _____ appears originate from a unique source of origin, and to distinguish its products or services from those of other entities. A _____ is a type of intellectual property, and typically a name, word, phrase, logo, symbol, design, image, or a combination of these elements. There is also a range of non-conventional _____s comprising marks which do not fall into these standard categories.
   a. Power III
   b. Risk management
   c. 180SearchAssistant
   d. Trademark

8. _____ is a violation of the exclusive rights attaching to a trademark without the authorization of the trademark owner or any licensees (provided that such authorization was within the scope of the license.) Infringement may occur when one party, the 'infringer', uses a trademark which is identical or confusingly similar to a trademark owned by another party, in relation to products or services which are identical or similar to the products or services which the registration covers. An owner of a trademark may commence legal proceedings against a party which infringes its registration.
   a. Passing off
   b. Trademark classification
   c. Fair Debt Collection Practices Act
   d. Trademark Infringement

9. _____ is the unauthorized use of material that is covered by copyright law, in a manner that violates one of the copyright owner's exclusive rights, such as the right to reproduce or perform the copyrighted work, or to make derivative works.

For electronic and audio-visual media, unauthorized reproduction and distribution is occasionally referred to as piracy. The practice of labeling the act of infringement as 'piracy' actually predates copyright itself.

   a. Patent
   b. Mediation
   c. Non-conventional trademark
   d. Copyright infringement

10. _____ is a sub-discipline and type of marketing. There are two main definitional characteristics which distinguish it from other types of marketing. The first is that it attempts to send its messages directly to consumers, without the use of intervening media.
   a. Power III
   b. Direct marketing
   c. Direct Marketing Associations
   d. Database marketing

Chapter 7. Online Marketing

11. _____ is a form of direct marketing which uses electronic mail as a means of communicating commercial or fundraising messages to an audience. In its broadest sense, every e-mail sent to a potential or current customer could be considered _____. However, the term is usually used to refer to:

- sending e-mails with the purpose of enhancing the relationship of a merchant with its current or previous customers and to encourage customer loyalty and repeat business,
- sending e-mails with the purpose of acquiring new customers or convincing current customers to purchase something immediately,
- adding advertisements to e-mails sent by other companies to their customers, and
- sending e-mails over the Internet, as e-mail did and does exist outside the Internet (e.g., network e-mail and FIDO.)

Researchers estimate that United States firms alone spent US$400 million on _____ in 2006.

_____ is popular with companies for several reasons:

- A mailing list provides the ability to distribute information to a wide range of specific, potential customers at a relatively low cost.
- Compared to other media investments such as direct mail or printed newsletters, e-mail is less expensive.
- An exact return on investment can be tracked ('track to basket') and has proven to be high when done properly. _____ is often reported as second only to search marketing as the most effective online marketing tactic.
- The delivery time for an e-mail message is short (i.e., seconds or minutes) as compared to a mailed advertisement (i.e., one or more days.)
- An advertiser is able to 'push' the message to its audience, as opposed to website-based advertising, which relies on a customer to visit that website.
- It is possible to impress the target audience using various unique fonts and formats. This will help in making the email messages more appealing and sweet.
- E-mail messages are easy to track. An advertiser can track users via autoresponders, web bugs, bounce messages, unsubscribe requests, read receipts, click-throughs, etc. These mechanisms can be used to measure open rates, positive or negative responses, and to correlate sales with marketing.
- Advertisers can generate repeat business affordably and automatically.
- Advertisers can reach substantial numbers of e-mail subscribers who have opted in (i.e., consented) to receive e-mail communications on subjects of interest to them.
- Over half of Internet users check or send e-mail on a typical day.
- Specific types of interaction with messages can trigger (1) other messages to be delivered automatically, or (2) other events, such as updating the profile of the recipient to indicate a specific interest category.
- _____ is paper-free (i.e., 'green'.)

Many companies use _____ to communicate with existing customers, but many other companies send unsolicited bulk e-mail, also known as spam.

Internet system administrators have always considered themselves responsible for dealing with 'abuse of the net', but not 'abuse on the net'.

a. Audience Screening
b. Enterprise Search Marketing
c. Online shopping rewards
d. E-mail marketing

12. _____ is an advertisement in which a particular product specifically mentions a competitor by name for the express purpose of showing why the competitor is inferior to the product naming it.

This should not be confused with parody advertisements, where a fictional product is being advertised for the purpose of poking fun at the particular advertisement, nor should it be confused with the use of a coined brand name for the purpose of comparing the product without actually naming an actual competitor. ('Wikipedia tastes better and is less filling than the Encyclopedia Galactica.')

In the 1980s, during what has been referred to as the cola wars, soft-drink manufacturer Pepsi ran a series of advertisements where people, caught on hidden camera, in a blind taste test, chose Pepsi over rival Coca-Cola.

a. Heavy-up
b. GL-70
c. Comparative advertising
d. Cost per conversion

13. A _____ is an entity that provides services to other entities. Usually this refers to a business that provides subscription or web service to other businesses or individuals. Examples of these services include Internet access, Mobile phone operator, and web application hosting.
a. Service provider
b. Yield management
c. Cross-selling
d. Freebie marketing

14. _____ is a form of communication that typically attempts to persuade potential customers to purchase or to consume more of a particular brand of product or service. 'While now central to the contemporary global economy and the reproduction of global production networks, it is only quite recently that _____ has been more than a marginal influence on patterns of sales and production. The formation of modern _____ was intimately bound up with the emergence of new forms of monopoly capitalism around the end of the 19th and beginning of the 20th century as one element in corporate strategies to create, organize and where possible control markets, especially for mass produced consumer goods.

Chapter 7. Online Marketing

a. AMAX
b. Advertising
c. ADTECH
d. ACNielsen

15. The _____, commonly referred to as HP, is a technology corporation headquartered in Palo Alto, California, United States. HP is the largest technology company in the world and operates in nearly every country. HP specializes in developing and manufacturing computing, storage, and networking hardware, software and services.

a. Hewlett-Packard Company
b. Power III
c. 6-3-5 Brainwriting
d. 180SearchAssistant

16. _____, small print, or 'mouseprint' is less noticeable print smaller than the more obvious larger print it accompanies that advertises or otherwise describes or partially describes a commercial product or service. The larger print that is used in conjunction with _____ is generally ingenuously used by the merchant to, in effect, deceive the consumer into believing the offer is more advantageous than it really is, via a legal technicality which requires full disclosure of all (even unfavorable) terms or conditions, but does not specify the manner (size, typeface, coloring, etc.) of disclosure.

a. Power III
b. Misleading advertising
c. Fine print
d. False advertising

17. _____ describes activities of businesses serving end consumers with products and/or services.

An example of a B2C transaction would be a person buying a pair of shoes from a retailer. The transactions that led to the shoes being available for purchase, that is the purchase of the leather, laces, rubber, etc.

a. Corporate capabilities package
b. Demand generation
c. Societal marketing
d. Business-to-consumer

18. _____ is a broad label that refers to any individuals or households that use goods and services generated within the economy. The concept of a _____ is used in different contexts, so that the usage and significance of the term may vary.

A _____ is a person who uses any product or service.

Chapter 7. Online Marketing

a. Power III
b. 6-3-5 Brainwriting
c. 180SearchAssistant
d. Consumer

19. Electronic commerce, commonly known as _____ or eCommerce, consists of the buying and selling of products or services over electronic systems such as the Internet and other computer networks. The amount of trade conducted electronically has grown extraordinarily with wide-spread Internet usage. A wide variety of commerce is conducted in this way, spurring and drawing on innovations in electronic funds transfer, supply chain management, Internet marketing, online transaction processing, electronic data interchange (EDI), inventory management systems, and automated data collection systems.
   a. AMAX
   b. ADTECH
   c. ACNielsen
   d. E-commerce

20. The most important feature of a contract is that one party makes an _____ for an arrangement that another accepts. This can be called a 'concurrence of wills' or 'ad idem' (meeting of the minds) of two or more parties. The concept is somewhat contested.
   a. AMAX
   b. Offer
   c. ADTECH
   d. ACNielsen

21. _____ (or citizen-to-citizen) electronic commerce involves the electronically-facilitated transactions between consumers through some third party. A common example is the online auction, in which a consumer posts an item for sale and other consumers bid to purchase it; the third party generally charges a flat fee or commission. The sites are only intermediaries, just there to match consumers.
   a. Consumer-to-consumer
   b. Web banner
   c. Business-to-government
   d. Locator software

22. The _____ is a compilation and codification of the general and permanent federal law of the United States. It contains 50 titles and is published every six years by the Office of the Law Revision Counsel of the US House of Representatives.

The official text of an Act of Congress is that of the 'enrolled bill' (traditionally printed on parchment) presented to the President for his signature or disapproval.

a. ADTECH
b. ACNielsen
c. AMAX
d. United States Code

23. The verb _____ or grant _____ means to give permission. The noun _____ refers to that permission as well as to the document memorializing that permission. _____ may be granted by a party to another party as an element of an agreement between those parties.

a. 6-3-5 Brainwriting
b. 180SearchAssistant
c. License
d. Power III

24. _____, a form of alternative dispute resolution (ADR), is a legal technique for the resolution of disputes outside the courts, wherein the parties to a dispute refer it to one or more persons (the 'arbitrators', 'arbiters' or 'arbitral tribunal'), by whose decision (the 'award') they agree to be bound. It is a settlement technique in which a third party reviews the case and imposes a decision that is legally binding for both sides. Other forms of ADR include mediation (a form of settlement negotiation facilitated by a neutral third party) and non-binding resolution by experts.

a. ACNielsen
b. Arbitration
c. AMAX
d. ADTECH

Chapter 8. Consumer Protection and Privacy Issues

1. _____ is a broad label that refers to any individuals or households that use goods and services generated within the economy. The concept of a _____ is used in different contexts, so that the usage and significance of the term may vary.

A _____ is a person who uses any product or service.

   a. 6-3-5 Brainwriting
   b. Consumer
   c. Power III
   d. 180SearchAssistant

2. _____ is a form of communication that typically attempts to persuade potential customers to purchase or to consume more of a particular brand of product or service. 'While now central to the contemporary global economy and the reproduction of global production networks, it is only quite recently that _____ has been more than a marginal influence on patterns of sales and production. The formation of modern _____ was intimately bound up with the emergence of new forms of monopoly capitalism around the end of the 19th and beginning of the 20th century as one element in corporate strategies to create, organize and where possible control markets, especially for mass produced consumer goods.
   a. AMAX
   b. Advertising
   c. ACNielsen
   d. ADTECH

3. False advertising or _____ is the use of false or misleading statements in advertising. As advertising has the potential to persuade people into commercial transactions that they might otherwise avoid, many governments around the world use regulations to control false, deceptive or misleading advertising. Truth in labeling refers to essentially the same concept, that customers have the right to know what they are buying, and that all necessary information should be on the label.
   a. Misleading advertising
   b. Power III
   c. Deceptive advertising
   d. Fine print

4. The _____ is an independent agency of the United States government, established in 1914 by the _____ Act. Its principal mission is the promotion of 'consumer protection' and the elimination and prevention of what regulators perceive to be harmfully 'anti-competitive' business practices, such as coercive monopoly.

The _____ Act was one of President Wilson's major acts against trusts.

a. 6-3-5 Brainwriting
b. Federal Trade Commission
c. Power III
d. 180SearchAssistant

5. The _____ of 1914 (15 U.S.C §§ 41-58, as amended) established the Federal Trade Commission (FTC), a bipartisan body of five members appointed by the President of the United States for seven year terms. This Commission was authorized to issue Cease and Desist orders to large corporations to curb unfair trade practices. This Act also gave more flexibility to the US congress for judicial matters.
   a. Federal Trade Commission Act
   b. Comparative negligence
   c. Gripe site
   d. Product liability

6. _____ as a legal term refers to promotional statements and claims that express subjective rather than objective views, such that no reasonable person would take literally. _____ is especially featured in testimonials.

In a legal context, the term originated in the English Court of Appeal case Carlill v Carbolic Smoke Ball Company, which centred on whether a monetary reimbursement should be paid when an influenza preventative device failed to work.

   a. Heinz pickle pin
   b. Conquesting
   c. Custom media
   d. Puffery

7. The United States _____ is an independent agency of the United States government created in 1972 through the Consumer Product Safety Act to protect 'against unreasonable risks of injuries associated with consumer products.' As of 2006 its acting chairman is Nancy Nord, a Republican. The other commissioner is Thomas Hill Moore, a Democrat. Normally the board has three commissioners.
   a. 180SearchAssistant
   b. Power III
   c. Consumer Product Safety Commission
   d. 6-3-5 Brainwriting

Chapter 8. Consumer Protection and Privacy Issues

8. The _____ is a very large set of interlinked hypertext documents accessed via the Internet. With a Web browser, one can view Web pages that may contain text, images, videos, and other multimedia and navigate between them using hyperlinks. Using concepts from earlier hypertext systems, the _____ was begun in 1992 by the English physicist Sir Tim Berners-Lee, now the Director of the _____ Consortium, and Robert Cailliau, a Belgian computer scientist, while both were working at CERN in Geneva, Switzerland.

   a. 180SearchAssistant
   b. 6-3-5 Brainwriting
   c. Power III
   d. World Wide Web

9. _____ is a form of government regulation which protects the interests of consumers. For example, a government may require businesses to disclose detailed information about products--particularly in areas where safety or public health is an issue, such as food. _____ is linked to the idea of consumer rights (that consumers have various rights as consumers), and to the formation of consumer organizations which help consumers make better choices in the marketplace.

   a. Sound trademark
   b. Federal Bureau of Investigation
   c. Trademark dilution
   d. Consumer Protection

10. _____ is defined by the American _____ Association as the activity, set of institutions, and processes for creating, communicating, delivering, and exchanging offerings that have value for customers, clients, partners, and society at large. The term developed from the original meaning which referred literally to going to market, as in shopping, or going to a market to sell goods or services.

    _____ practice tends to be seen as a creative industry, which includes advertising, distribution and selling.

   a. Marketing myopia
   b. Marketing
   c. Product naming
   d. Customer acquisition management

11. _____ is a method of direct marketing in which a salesperson solicits to prospective customers to buy products or services, either over the phone or through a subsequent face to face or Web conferencing appointment scheduled during the call.

    _____ can also include recorded sales pitches programmed to be played over the phone via automatic dialing. _____ has come under fire in recent years, being viewed as an annoyance by many.

a. Directory Harvest Attack
b. Telemarketing
c. Joe job
d. Phishing

12. Merchandising refers to the methods, practices and operations conducted to promote and sustain certain categories of commercial activity. The term is understood to have different specific meanings depending on the context. _____ is a sale goods at a store

In marketing, one of the definitions of merchandising is the practice in which the brand or image from one product or service is used to sell another.

a. Sales promotion
b. Merchandising
c. Merchandise
d. New Media Strategies

13. _____ networking is a method of delivering computer network services in which the participants share a portion of their own resources, such as processing power, disk storage, network bandwidth, printing facilities. Such resources are provided directly to other participants without intermediary network hosts or servers. _____ network participants are providers and consumers of network services simultaneously, which contrasts with other service models, such as traditional client-server computing.

a. Power III
b. 180SearchAssistant
c. 6-3-5 Brainwriting
d. Peer-to-peer

14. A _____ or trade mark, identified by the symbols â„¢ (not yet registered) and Â® (registered) business organization or other legal entity to identify that the products and/or services to consumers with which the _____ appears originate from a unique source of origin, and to distinguish its products or services from those of other entities. A _____ is a type of intellectual property, and typically a name, word, phrase, logo, symbol, design, image, or a combination of these elements. There is also a range of non-conventional _____s comprising marks which do not fall into these standard categories.

a. Trademark
b. 180SearchAssistant
c. Risk management
d. Power III

Chapter 8. Consumer Protection and Privacy Issues

15. The _____ is a United States federal law (15 U.S.C. § 2301 et seq.). Enacted in 1975, it is the federal statute that governs warranties on consumer products.

The statute is remedial in nature and is intended to protect consumers from deceptive warranty practices. Consumer products are not required to have warranties, but if one is given, it must comply with the _____.

   a. Singapore Treaty on the Law of Trademarks
   b. Community Trade Mark
   c. Confusing similarity
   d. Magnuson-Moss Warranty Act

16. _____, small print, or 'mouseprint' is less noticeable print smaller than the more obvious larger print it accompanies that advertises or otherwise describes or partially describes a commercial product or service . The larger print that is used in conjunction with _____ is generally ingenuously used by the merchant to, in effect, deceive the consumer into believing the offer is more advantageous than it really is, via a legal technicality which requires full disclosure of all (even unfavorable) terms or conditions, but does not specify the manner (size, typeface, coloring, etc.) of disclosure.
   a. Power III
   b. False advertising
   c. Misleading advertising
   d. Fine print

17. A personal and cultural _____ is a relative ethic _____, an assumption upon which implementation can be extrapolated. A _____ system is a set of consistent _____s and measures that is soo not true. A principle _____ is a foundation upon which other _____s and measures of integrity are based.
   a. Value
   b. Perceptual maps
   c. Supreme Court of the United States
   d. Package-on-Package

18. In economics, business, retail, and accounting, a _____ is the value of money that has been used up to produce something, and hence is not available for use anymore. In economics, a _____ is an alternative that is given up as a result of a decision. In business, the _____ may be one of acquisition, in which case the amount of money expended to acquire it is counted as _____.
   a. Cost
   b. Variable cost
   c. Fixed costs
   d. Transaction cost

19. In economic models, the _____ time frame assumes no fixed factors of production. Firms can enter or leave the marketplace, and the cost (and availability) of land, labor, raw materials, and capital goods can be assumed to vary. In contrast, in the short-run time frame, certain factors are assumed to be fixed, because there is not sufficient time for them to change.
   a. Power III
   b. 6-3-5 Brainwriting
   c. 180SearchAssistant
   d. Long-run

20. The _____ is the primary unit in the United States Department of Justice, serving as both a federal criminal investigative body and a domestic intelligence agency. The FBI has investigative jurisdiction over violations of more than 200 categories of federal crime. Its motto is 'Fidelity, Bravery, Integrity,' corresponding to the 'FBI' initialism.
   a. Trademark dilution
   b. Federal Bureau of Investigation
   c. Foreign Corrupt Practices Act
   d. Service mark

21. _____ is the ability of an individual or group to seclude themselves or information about themselves and thereby reveal themselves selectively. The boundaries and content of what is considered private differ among cultures and individuals, but share basic common themes. _____ is sometimes related to anonymity, the wish to remain unnoticed or unidentified in the public realm.
   a. Power III
   b. 180SearchAssistant
   c. Privacy
   d. 6-3-5 Brainwriting

22. _____ is the area of law concerned with the protection and preservation of the privacy rights of individuals. Increasingly, governments and other public as well as private organizations collect vast amounts of personal information about individuals for a variety of purposes. The law of privacy regulates the type of information which may be collected and how this information may be used.
   a. Madrid system
   b. Collective mark
   c. Trademark attorney
   d. Privacy law

Chapter 8. Consumer Protection and Privacy Issues

23. _____ is a form of intellectual property which gives the creator of an original work exclusive rights for a certain time period in relation to that work, including its publication, distribution and adaptation; after which time the work is said to enter the public domain. _____ applies to any expressible form of an idea or information that is substantive and discrete. Some jurisdictions also recognize 'moral rights' of the creator of a work, such as the right to be credited for the work.
    a. Reasonable person standard
    b. Collective mark
    c. Celler-Kefauver Act
    d. Copyright

24. _____, commonly known as e-commerce or eCommerce, consists of the buying and selling of products or services over electronic systems such as the Internet and other computer networks. The amount of trade conducted electronically has grown extraordinarily with wide-spread Internet usage. A wide variety of commerce is conducted in this way, spurring and drawing on innovations in electronic funds transfer, supply chain management, Internet marketing, online transaction processing, electronic data interchange (EDI), inventory management systems, and automated data collection systems.
    a. ACNielsen
    b. AMAX
    c. ADTECH
    d. Electronic Commerce

25. _____ are legal property rights over creations of the mind, both artistic and commercial, and the corresponding fields of law. Under _____ law, owners are granted certain exclusive rights to a variety of intangible assets, such as musical, literary, and artistic works; ideas, discoveries and inventions; and words, phrases, symbols, and designs. Common types of _____ include copyrights, trademarks, patents, industrial design rights and trade secrets.
    a. ACNielsen
    b. Elasticity
    c. Opinion leadership
    d. Intellectual property

26. _____ (or citizen-to-citizen) electronic commerce involves the electronically-facilitated transactions between consumers through some third party. A common example is the online auction, in which a consumer posts an item for sale and other consumers bid to purchase it; the third party generally charges a flat fee or commission. The sites are only intermediaries, just there to match consumers.
    a. Web banner
    b. Consumer-to-consumer
    c. Locator software
    d. Business-to-government

Chapter 8. Consumer Protection and Privacy Issues

27. The _____ is an American federal law (codified at 15 U.S.C. § 1681 et seq.) that regulates the collection, dissemination, and use of consumer credit information.
    a. 180SearchAssistant
    b. Power III
    c. 6-3-5 Brainwriting
    d. Fair Credit Reporting Act

28. _____ is an advertisement in which a particular product specifically mentions a competitor by name for the express purpose of showing why the competitor is inferior to the product naming it.

    This should not be confused with parody advertisements, where a fictional product is being advertised for the purpose of poking fun at the particular advertisement, nor should it be confused with the use of a coined brand name for the purpose of comparing the product without actually naming an actual competitor. ('Wikipedia tastes better and is less filling than the Encyclopedia Galactica.')

    In the 1980s, during what has been referred to as the cola wars, soft-drink manufacturer Pepsi ran a series of advertisements where people, caught on hidden camera, in a blind taste test, chose Pepsi over rival Coca-Cola.

    a. Heavy-up
    b. Cost per conversion
    c. GL-70
    d. Comparative advertising

29. _____ is a technique used in propaganda and advertising. Also known as association, this is a technique of projecting positive or negative qualities (praise or blame) of a person, entity, object, or value (an individual, group, organization, nation, patriotism, etc.) to another in order to make the second more acceptable or to discredit it.
    a. Sexism,
    b. Supplier
    c. Micro ads
    d. Transfer

30. _____ refers to 'controlling human or societal behaviour by rules or restrictions.' _____ can take many forms: legal restrictions promulgated by a government authority, self-_____, social _____, co-_____ and market _____. One can consider _____ as actions of conduct imposing sanctions (such as a fine.) This action of administrative law, or implementing regulatory law, may be contrasted with statutory or case law.

Chapter 8. Consumer Protection and Privacy Issues

a. Rule of four
b. CAN-SPAM
c. Non-conventional trademark
d. Regulation

31. _____, also referred to as i-marketing, web marketing, online marketing is the marketing of products or services over the Internet.

The Internet has brought many unique benefits to marketing, one of which being lower costs for the distribution of information and media to a global audience. The interactive nature of _____, both in terms of providing instant response and eliciting responses, is a unique quality of the medium.

a. Internet marketing
b. AMAX
c. ACNielsen
d. ADTECH

32. _____ is a type of advertising whereby advertisements are placed so as to reach consumers based on various traits such as demographics, purchase history, or observed behavior.

Two principal forms of targeted interactive advertising are behavioral targeting and contextual advertising.

a. Targeted advertising
b. Brand parity
c. Specialty catalogs
d. Sugging

33. A _____ is a statement or claim that a particular event will occur in the future in more certain terms than a forecast. The etymology of this word is Latin . In regards to predicting the future Howard H. Stevenson Says, ' _____ is at least two things: Important and hard.' Important, because we have to act, and hard because we have to realize the future we want, and what is the best way to get there.

a. 180SearchAssistant
b. Power III
c. 6-3-5 Brainwriting
d. Prediction

Chapter 8. Consumer Protection and Privacy Issues

34. _____ is a sub-discipline and type of marketing. There are two main definitional characteristics which distinguish it from other types of marketing. The first is that it attempts to send its messages directly to consumers, without the use of intervening media.
    a. Database marketing
    b. Power III
    c. Direct marketing
    d. Direct Marketing Associations

35. _____ is a term commonly used to describe commerce transactions between businesses like the one between a manufacturer and a wholesaler or a wholesaler and a retailer i.e both the buyer and the seller are business entity.This is unlike business-to-consumers (B2C) which involve a business entity and end consumer, or business-to-government (B2G) which involve a business entity and government.

    The volume of B2B transactions is much higher than the volume of B2C transactions. The primary reason for this is that in a typical supply chain there will be many B2B transactions involving subcomponent or raw materials, and only one B2C transaction, specifically sale of the finished product to the end customer.

    a. Social marketing
    b. Disruptive technology
    c. Business-to-business
    d. Customer relationship management

36. _____ is an independent, privately held organization best known for its Web Privacy Seal. _____ runs the world's largest privacy seal program, with more than 2,000 Web sites certified, including the major internet portals and leading brands such as IBM, Oracle Corporation, Intuit and eBay. _____ states its purpose is to establish trusting relationships between individuals and online organizations based on respect for personal identity and information in the evolving networked world.
    a. Power III
    b. 6-3-5 Brainwriting
    c. 180SearchAssistant
    d. TRUSTe

37. The _____, commonly referred to as HP, is a technology corporation headquartered in Palo Alto, California, United States. HP is the largest technology company in the world and operates in nearly every country. HP specializes in developing and manufacturing computing, storage, and networking hardware, software and services.

a. 180SearchAssistant
b. Power III
c. Hewlett-Packard Company
d. 6-3-5 Brainwriting

ANSWER KEY

Chapter 1
1. d   2. b   3. d   4. a   5. d   6. d   7. d   8. d   9. d   10. d
11. b   12. d   13. c   14. d   15. d   16. d   17. d   18. b   19. d   20. d
21. b   22. d   23. d   24. c

Chapter 2
1. d   2. d   3. d   4. d   5. a   6. c   7. d   8. d   9. d   10. d
11. b   12. d   13. d   14. c   15. b   16. a   17. c   18. c   19. d   20. b

Chapter 3
1. a   2. d   3. c   4. d   5. a   6. d   7. d   8. a   9. d   10. d
11. b   12. d   13. c   14. d   15. d   16. d   17. d   18. b   19. d   20. d
21. d   22. d

Chapter 4
1. c   2. d   3. d   4. d   5. d   6. d   7. b   8. d   9. a   10. d
11. d   12. d   13. c   14. d   15. d   16. b   17. b   18. d   19. d   20. c
21. d   22. c   23. c   24. d   25. d   26. c   27. b   28. c   29. b   30. d
31. c   32. b   33. d   34. a   35. a   36. d   37. d   38. d   39. d   40. b
41. a

Chapter 5
1. a   2. d   3. d   4. d   5. a   6. c   7. d   8. a   9. c   10. c
11. d   12. d   13. d   14. b   15. a   16. d   17. c   18. d   19. d   20. c
21. d   22. c   23. b   24. b   25. c

Chapter 6
1. d   2. c   3. b   4. d   5. d   6. d   7. a   8. d   9. c   10. a
11. c   12. d   13. d   14. d   15. d   16. d   17. d   18. a   19. b   20. d
21. d   22. d   23. b   24. a   25. d   26. a   27. c   28. c   29. b

Chapter 7
1. c   2. b   3. a   4. d   5. a   6. b   7. d   8. d   9. d   10. b
11. d   12. c   13. a   14. b   15. a   16. c   17. d   18. d   19. d   20. b
21. a   22. d   23. c   24. b

Chapter 8
1. b   2. b   3. c   4. b   5. a   6. d   7. c   8. d   9. d   10. b
11. b   12. c   13. d   14. a   15. d   16. d   17. a   18. a   19. d   20. b
21. c   22. d   23. d   24. d   25. d   26. b   27. d   28. d   29. d   30. d
31. a   32. a   33. d   34. c   35. c   36. d   37. c

www.ingramcontent.com/pod-product-compliance
Lightning Source LLC
Chambersburg PA
CBHW081850230426
43669CB00018B/2895